Cicero *Pro Milone*

The following titles are available from Bloomsbury for the OCR specifications in Latin and Greek, first teaching September 2016

Cicero *Pro Milone*: A Selection, with introduction by Lynn Fotheringham and commentary notes and vocabulary by Robert West

Ovid *Heroides*: A Selection, with introduction, commentary notes and vocabulary by John Godwin

Propertius, Tibullus and Ovid: A Selection of Love Poetry, with introduction, commentary notes and vocabulary by Anita Nikkanen

Seneca Letters: A Selection, with introduction, commentary notes and vocabulary by Eliot Maunder

Tacitus *Annals* I: A Selection, with introduction by Roland Mayer and commentary notes and vocabulary by Katharine Radice

Virgil *Aeneid* VIII: A Selection, with introduction, commentary notes and vocabulary by Keith Maclennan

Virgil *Aeneid* X: A Selection, with introduction, commentary notes and vocabulary by Christopher Tanfield

OCR Anthology for Classical Greek GCSE, covering the prescribed texts by Homer, Herodotus, Euripides, Lucian, Plato and Plutarch, edited by Judith Affleck and Clive Letchford

OCR Anthology for Classical Greek AS and A-level, covering the prescribed texts by Aristophanes, Homer, Plato, Sophocles, Thucydides and Xenophon, with introduction, commentary notes and vocabulary by Malcolm Campbell, Rob Colborn, Frederica Daniele, Ben Gravell, Sarah Harden, Steven Kennedy, Matthew McCullagh, Charlie Paterson, John Taylor and Claire Webster

Supplementary resources for these volumes can be found at www.bloomsbury.com/OCR-editions
Please type the URL into your web browser and follow the instructions to access the Companion Website. If you experience any problems, please contact Bloomsbury at contact@bloomsbury.com

Cicero *Pro Milone*:
A Selection

Sections 24–32, 34–35, 43–52, 53–64 (... *defendere*), 72–80

Commentary notes and vocabulary by Robert West
Introduction by Lynn Fotheringham

Bloomsbury Academic
An imprint of Bloomsbury Publishing Plc

B L O O M S B U R Y
LONDON · OXFORD · NEW YORK · NEW DELHI · SYDNEY

Bloomsbury Academic

An imprint of Bloomsbury Publishing Plc

50 Bedford Square	1385 Broadway
London	New York
WC1B 3DP	NY 10018
UK	USA

www.bloomsbury.com

BLOOMSBURY and the Diana logo are trademarks of Bloomsbury Publishing Plc

First published 2016
Reprinted 2016

Commentary notes and vocabulary © Robert West, 2016
Introduction © Lynn Fotheringham, 2016

Robert West and Lynn Fotheringham have asserted their rights under the Copyright, Designs and Patents Act, 1988, to be identified as Authors of this work.

British Library Cataloguing-in-Publication Data
A catalogue record for this book is available from the British Library.

ISBN:	PB:	978-1-47426-618-5
	ePub:	978-1-47426-619-2
	ePDF:	978-1-47426-620-8

Library of Congress Cataloging-in-Publication Data
A catalog record for this book is available from the Library of Congress.

Typeset by RefineCatch Limited, Bungay, Suffolk
Printed and bound in Great Britain

Contents

Preface

The text and notes found in this volume are designed to guide any student who has mastered Latin up to GCSE Level and wishes to read this text in the original.

The edition is, however, particularly designed to support students who are reading Cicero's speech in preparation for OCR's AS or A Level Latin examinations in 2017, 2018 and 2019. (Please note this edition uses AS to refer indiscriminately to AS and the expected first year of A Level, i.e. Group 1.)

The death of Publius Clodius and the prosecution of Milo for his murder came at a critical point in the history of the late Republic, with the Civil War between Caesar and Pompey, leading to the collapse of the Republic, only three years away. In his passionate defence of Milo, Cicero pleads for the rule of law as a vital counterweight to the anarchy that gang warfare on the streets of Rome had created. The published speech was regarded as a masterpiece of oratory in its own time, and is still held to be one of his finest compositions.

Lynn Fotheringham has provided a detailed introduction, setting the speech in its historical context and explaining, and illustrating, important features of Roman oratory. The commentary in the book and other supporting material to be found online are the work of Robert West. The notes to the speech aim to help students bridge the gap between GCSE and AS/A Level Latin, and they take full account of harder points of grammar and word order.

The commentary had its origins in an edition published privately by Robert West in 2006. He would like to repeat his thanks to many colleagues, pupils and friends (especially ARLT friends) who helped in its production, and in particular to Bradford Grammar School for a term's sabbatical leave and to Selwyn College, Cambridge, for accommodating him and providing study facilities in that term.

The text is based on (though not entirely identical with) the Oxford Classical Text of A. C. Clark. Teachers may like to try to track down a copy of Clark's magisterial commentary (1895), which has been invaluable in the compiling of this edition. *Praenomina* have been spelled out in full, not abbreviated as is conventional, to help and encourage those students and teachers who want to read sections of the speech aloud. At the end of the book is a full vocabulary list for all the words contained in the prescribed sections, with words in OCR's Defined Vocabulary List for AS Level Latin flagged by means of an asterisk.

Robert West
Lynn Fotheringham
September 2015

Introduction

The trial of Milo

Of all the judicial cases in which Cicero spoke for the defence, the trial of Titus Annius Milo in April 52 BC is the one about which we know the most. This is because, in addition to Cicero's speech, we have vivid accounts by several later writers of the events leading up to the trial, the trial itself and its aftermath; the reason these events were interesting was probably their politically controversial and highly dramatic nature. Two prominent politicians had become involved in a violent altercation on the Appian Way south of Rome, at a time when politics was characterized by frequent violence and even anarchy; one of the two had been killed. The dead man was the charismatic and controversial populist, Publius Clodius Pulcher; the survivor, Milo, had been publicly his enemy since they clashed, five years earlier, over whether or not Rome's greatest orator, Marcus Tullius Cicero, should be recalled from exile. As well as speaking in court for the defence, Cicero was therefore deeply enmeshed in the network of political enmities that formed the background of the case; these earlier events are discussed at *Mil.* 8, 34–9, 73, 78, 87, 89, 94, 102–3. And at the middle of the political whirlwind stood Rome's greatest general, Pompey the Great (Gnaeus Pompeius Magnus), apparently siding first with one side in this on-going feud, now with the other.

These events took place towards the end of the period known as the late Roman Republic. The oligarchical political system which had governed Rome since roughly the fifth century BC, after the expulsion of the kings, is often seen as already falling apart at this point in time; it would collapse completely in the next twenty-five years, replaced by the one-man rule of Augustus. For centuries the consuls, annually elected heads of state, had always been two in number; both the collegiate nature of the office and the fact that it was held for only a year ensured that too much power would never be concentrated in a single individual's hands. Public concern about such a concentration of power explains the controversies over the careers of both Pompey and Cicero. Pompey was a man of considerable military talent whose control of armies and popularity with the people had led to his holding a number of unprecedented and thoroughly unconstitutional military commands, although he conformed to the constitution by holding and then resigning the consulship, as was proper, in 70 and 55 BC. As was also proper, in both years he had had a colleague in the consulship, Marcus Licinius Crassus. But in the 50s BC he was known to be in a (sometimes uneasy) alliance with Crassus and Gaius Julius Caesar, which was seen by many in Rome's ruling body, the Senate, as a threat to the constitution.

Cicero had been elected to the consulship in 63 BC, probably due to the extensive networks of support brought to him by his oratorical skill. As consul he had arguably acted unconstitutionally when he countenanced the execution without trial of a group of men known as the Catilinarian conspirators; his consular colleague, Gaius Antonius, was an ineffectual man who was not considered responsible for this act. Cicero was attacked for having deprived Roman citizens of their judicial rights, and this was presented as the action of someone aiming at acquiring for himself more power than a single individual ought to be allowed to have. In 58 BC his enemy Clodius, with the connivance of Pompey, Caesar and Crassus, had passed a law threatening exile for anyone who had executed Roman citizens without trial, and Cicero had been forced to leave Rome. But a year later Clodius had apparently annoyed Pompey sufficiently for the latter to throw his weight behind the movement for Cicero's recall, a movement in which Milo had been a prime mover. Both Clodius and Milo were adept at organizing the poorer citizens into mobs; the threat of violence that had been bubbling under the surface of Roman politics for some years began to dominate political activity.

Four years after that, Milo was standing for election to the consulship of 52; Clodius, who was slightly younger, was standing for the less senior magistracy, the praetorship. The elections were continually postponed, due in part to the violence of the candidates. After Clodius' death, the chaos reached such a peak that even the most conservative in the Senate realized that something drastic had to be done. Pompey was invited to take charge, not as dictator – an office which had traditionally been used to allow one man to take the helm for a strictly limited period in times of crisis – but as consul without a colleague, an unheard-of position; Pompey surrounded himself with armed guards to an extent that would have been unusual, even illegal, in normal circumstances. This can be seen as foreshadowing the system of one-man rule that was to follow. He passed new laws under which Milo, and many others involved in the violence of the previous six months, were tried; he was present with his guards in the forum in order to ensure that Milo's trial would not be interrupted (*Mil.* 2–3, 71, 101). For a variety of reasons the defence was probably hopeless.

The sources agree that Cicero's performance was not his best, although different reasons are given. Milo was convicted and went into exile in Massilia (Marseille). In subsequent weeks several of Clodius' followers were also convicted. Justice seemed to be being dealt to both sides, or perhaps both factions were being purged. Cicero's speech for Milo must be read in the light of this on-going activity; its publication clearly did not commemorate a judicial victory. The trial was not, or not only, about justice, or even about justice being seen to be done, but about contesting the meaning of what had happened, the rights and wrongs of all parties. And this contest continued afterwards, in the later trials and no doubt in the public debates and private conversations of eminent Romans, and in their memoirs and histories and political pamphlets. It is likely that the published *Pro Milone*, which some later writers tell us was in any case not the same as the speech delivered in court, was intended to carry on the debate, to strike a blow in the (ultimately unsuccessful) fight for Milo's recall, and to give a definitive analysis of Clodius and his career.

Pompey eventually took a colleague in the consulship and elections for the following year took place as usual. But three years later he would be leading the senatorial forces in a civil war against Gaius Julius Caesar. The victorious Caesar made himself dictator, not on a temporary but a permanent basis. After his assassination in 44 BC, it was to take another thirteen years and more civil wars before there was only one man left standing: Caesar's nephew Octavian, known later as Augustus, who shunned the title 'dictator' and repeatedly held the consulship to give his power some form of legitimacy, but whose one-man rule was hardly concealed for all that: he appointed his own colleagues and successors. Writers in the imperial period looking back at the turbulent year of 52 BC might have seen Pompey as a forerunner of Augustus, and have been interested in the trial of Milo partly because of that.

To those involved at the time, the situation will have been interpreted in terms of the past. The conservative senators who came up with the novel consul-without-a-colleague position for Pompey probably wanted to avoid resorting to the office of dictator partly because of its association with Lucius Cornelius Sulla, who had held the position after marching his army on Rome itself in 88 and 82 BC. Pompey's whole career had been based on his control of an army, raised extra-legally to support Sulla in 83; he had already held a number of unprecedented positions of power. To the Romans, the word *rex* ('king') and the very idea of one-man rule was anathema, and a handy stick with which to beat political opponents; if Clodius accused Cicero of desiring it, Cicero was to accuse Clodius of the same. This shows how politicians directly opposed to one another could exploit the same language, making it difficult for us to associate specific accusations or slogans with different factions. All political behaviour was open to interpretation. Some people probably feared that Pompey was aiming at one-man rule; of his supporters, some may have believed that he was not, others may have felt (as many modern historians do) that the Republican system was no longer working and one-man rule was inevitable. Every aspect of politics was hotly contested at this period, which means that in spite of the amount of evidence we have, more than for almost any other period of the ancient world, it remains extremely difficult to see through the propaganda to anything like reality. The period is therefore no less challenging or interesting than one for which less evidence survives.

The later evidence must also be read in the light of the manifold contemporary debates, because it will have drawn on and been influenced by earlier, lost works which looked at the events from a variety of angles. Even the most neutral of the extant texts may depend on a far-from-neutral element in a contemporary discussion. Three principal authors provide us with information about the trial of Milo: Asconius, writing a commentary on the speech in the first century AD; Plutarch, writing a biography of Cicero in the late first/early second century AD; Cassius Dio, writing a history of Rome in the late second/early third century AD. The rhetorician Quintilian (late first century AD) also sheds occasional light. Asconius and Quintilian, both Romans, are positive about Cicero's oratory and generally also about the man himself. Of the others, both Greek, Plutarch strives for a balanced view; he has reasons for taking a positive attitude to Cicero but cannot escape noticing his flaws in the course of his narrative. Dio is known for anti-Ciceronian bias, but the space he gives to Cicero's actions suggests a fascination with him as a historical figure.

To the amount of evidence that survives for the trial itself and its context (including the evidence for the relationship between delivered and published versions), and to the drama and political significance of that context, must be added a third reason for the perennial fascination of this speech in particular: its quality. This, like everything else, is debated, but at least some ancient readers thought very highly of it. The speech also appears to correspond closely to the rhetorical handbooks on how speeches should be constructed, which makes possible an entertaining game of examining the correspondences and differences between practice and theory, and is also interesting because it is unusual at this point in Cicero's career. But before exploring that aspect of the speech, let us try to fill in a little more detail of the political background, so essential to understanding what Cicero is trying to do. To this account many more sources than those listed above necessarily contribute.

Late Republican politics

The political situation at Rome in the late Republic was filled with anxiety. To set the scene for the 60s and 50s BC, it is necessary to consider two earlier sequences of events. The first, which Cicero refers to several times over the course of the speech, begins with the tribunate of Tiberius Sempronius Gracchus in 133 BC. Apparently moved by the plight of the peasant-farmers of Italy, constantly conscripted into the Roman army and losing their small-holdings to wealthy men buying up extensive estates, he proposed land-reform. The magistracy he held as tribune of the plebs was traditionally associated with defending the 'people' against the autocracy of the wealthy, even although the ancient distinction between patricians and plebeians was no longer of much importance: numerous plebeian families had entered the ranks of the aristocracy, now known as *nobiles* ('noblemen') whether of patrician or plebeian origin. Anyone with an ancestor who had held the consulship was a *nobilis*. The body Gracchus described himself as defending could be referred to as the *plebs* or the *populus* ('people'), his tactics could be described as *popularis*.

The idea of land-reform led many of the Senate, who were all wealthy, to look on Gracchus as a dangerous revolutionary; he exacerbated the situation by standing for the tribunate two years in a row, and by forcing out of office another tribune who attempted to oppose him (*Mil.* 72). These actions could be presented as giving him an unparalleled amount of power; he was accused of aiming at monarchy, which may have been largely a tactic to discredit him among the *populus* of which he represented himself a champion. When one of the consuls refused to take violent action against him, the Pontifex Maximus, Scipio Nasica (*Mil.* 8, 14, 83) led a senatorial lynch-mob which put an end to Tiberius' life and his programme. Twelve years later his younger brother Gaius, attempting to revive that programme, suffered a similar fate. The Senate passed a decree saying something like 'let the consuls take action so that the state takes no harm' (*consules darent operam ne quid detrimenti res publica caperet*); this decree, referred to by modern historians as the *senatus consultum ultimum* ('final' or 'last-resort decree of the Senate') or *s.c.u.*, was interpreted as sanctioning the use of violence. The consul Opimius (*Mil.* 8, 14, 83), accompanied by a band of Cretan archers attached to the army, led the senatorial opposition against Gaius, who was killed. These events were shocking, and arguably changed the atmosphere of Roman politics. Those putting forward legislation more favourable to the mass of the people than to the Senate had been shown what a risk they might be taking; violence within the city itself had been perpetrated by the Senate.

All active politicians were necessarily wealthy men and most were of elite descent. After the Gracchi, those who showed more concern than others for the mass of the poorer citizens, whether genuinely or as a tactic to increase their own political power by gaining the popular vote, were referred to by their opponents in the Senate as *populares*.

While some of them sometimes worked together, they did not constitute anything like a political party in the modern sense, or even a coherent faction; they were a series of men, or of groups of men, who employed similar political tactics – the courting of the *populus* – and espoused a similar set of policies because of what the *populus* was assumed to want. Against these is often set another group, referred to as 'conservatives', 'the senatorial party', or '*optimates*'; the last word is related to *optimus*, 'best'. Instead of courting the *populus*, this group is seen as depending on the support of fellow senators, especially the old senatorial families, and as opposed to change of all kinds, including the exercise of power by anyone other than themselves. In his speech *Pro Sestio* Cicero defines the term *optimates* more broadly as encompassing not just the traditional 'best men', the elite families, but all Romans, of whatever origin or station, who wish the best for the state. Cicero is polemical here, but the speech is another reminder of the essential flexibility of political language, and therefore of its unreliability as a clear historical indicator of particular attitudes and factions. The word *popularis* is problematic too, because it can mean simply 'popular'; Cicero himself claimed to be a *consul populis* during his consulship.

Although it has long been recognized that the *optimates* and *populares* were not 'parties', the continuing tendency to label some politicians and policies 'optimate' and others 'popular' means that political disagreements in the late Republic are still presented as resembling those between modern political parties, straightforwardly polarized between conservative and radical. Some individuals who seem to have favoured different extremes at different times, notably Pompey and Cicero, are perhaps too readily accused of inconsistency, when in fact they and many others may have voted not according to a 'party line' but on the issues, taking now a stance that appears to be closer to one extreme, now one closer to the other, without feeling any sense of inconsistency.

In the *Pro Milone*, Cicero uses the adjective *popularis* only once, in a negative sense (*Mil.* 22), but his frequent references to the *populus Romanus* are all positive. He never uses the noun *optimates*, but does describe several individuals as *optimus*; we have seen that he was capable of using even the more technical political term to encompass more than the old elite. He is not leaning heavily on the *optimates–popularis* polarity, but rather on the polarity between good and wicked; see for example the characterization of Clodius at *Mil.* 24 and *passim*. There is no acknowledgement of the possibility that the honest but less well-off citizens might have had good reasons to support Clodius' policies, which are always described as aimed at gathering the support of the criminal or insane, or even worse, slaves (*Mil.* 87); the Roman people are always on Milo's side, and on Cicero's (*Mil.* 3, 39). Although this may have been blatant misrepresentation or simply fantasy, there had been times in the past when the vast majority of the Roman people had been on Cicero's side, even against Clodius (*Mil.* 39, 73); in all the speeches after his return from exile (see 'A *popularis* agitator and his opponent: Clodius and Milo'), he works hard to represent this state of affairs as reflecting the true opinion of all honest citizens.

The second sequence of events which increased political anxiety and specifically the fear of violence was the conflict between Marius and Sulla. In 88 BC, as consul, Sulla was assigned command of the war against a Greek king in Asia Minor, Mithridates VI of Pontus, by the Senate in the normal way; the command was subsequently taken away from Sulla by a vote of the people, stirred up by a tribune acting on behalf of his rival Marius. Rather than comply, he marched his army on Rome, then departed for the East, effectively leaving the city to the Marians, who took it back with considerable bloodshed only ended by the sudden death of Marius. Sulla wrapped up the war by 83 BC and returned to Italy to face civil war, which he won. Established as dictator *legibus faciendis et rei publicae constituendae* ('to make laws and to

organize/ensure the continued well-being of the state'), he introduced
a range of constitutional reforms to strengthen the authority of the
Senate (82–80 BC). Unlike most of the other warlords of the first
century BC, he was aligned more with the Senate than with the
populus. He severely curtailed the power of the tribunate, enlarged
the Senate and increased the number of annual magistrates. These
measures presumably aimed to ensure that most individuals held less
power, acquired it less quickly and could hold on to it less easily.
Unfortunately the example of his own unconstitutional use of military
might was more powerful than the constitution he established, which
was in any case gradually dismantled over the next few years. The fear
that another general might decide to do the same as Sulla had done
never went away.

Optimates or *populares*? Pompey and Cicero

Pompey and Cicero were both born in 106 BC. Both came from Italian
towns outside Rome itself, although Pompey's father had held the
consulship, rendering his descendants *nobiles*, considered worthy of
holding the magistracy themselves. But in fact Pompey's power always
lay outside traditional and constitutional politics. In the *Pro Milone*
Cicero must not emphasize this aspect of Pompey's career, but rather
expresses his extraordinary status in terms of his importance to the
state (*Mil.* 18–19, 65–6, 70–1). Although he came to prominence as a
supporter of Sulla in 83 BC, with an army he raised himself, his career
was an affront to the Sullan constitution. Only consuls and praetors
were supposed to hold *imperium* (military command), when in their
late thirties/early forties, after holding a series of preliminary
magistracies. Pompey was in his twenties and had held no magistracies
at all, but his *imperium* was simply a fact, and nothing could be done
about it. When in 71 BC he declared his intention of standing for the

consulship, he was still seven years younger than the required age and had held none of the previous magistracies. But his desire for the office may have been intended, or understood, as a sign that he wished to comply more closely with the constitution, acquiring a cloak of pseudo-legality to cover his naked use of military-based power. Immensely popular, whether *popularis* or not, he was easily elected for the year 70 BC along with his lifelong rival Crassus, another former supporter of Sulla's; the two of them proceeded to pass legislation undoing several of Sulla's reforms, including the restrictions on the power of the tribunate.

Cicero on the other hand was a *novus homo* ('new man'), whose ancestors had held no magistracies whatsoever at Rome, and he had little military inclination. Cicero's talent was for oratory. He made a splash on the political scene just before Sulla's retirement by defending Sextus Roscius of Ameria, accused of parricide in 80 BC; Cicero presents Roscius as the innocent victim of a conspiracy involving one of Sulla's freedmen, but is careful to exonerate Sulla himself. He spent the next decade developing his oratorical ability and using judicial activity to build up a network of supporters, perhaps especially among the equestrian (wealthy non-senatorial) class and the Italians now holding the franchise at Rome. Remarkable success crowned his efforts inasmuch as he ran successfully for election to each of the four major magistracies in the first year he was qualified to do so; these successes, as well as his recall from exile in 57 BC, underpin his claims to be beloved by the Roman people at, e.g. *Mil.* 5, 12, 34, 39. In 70 BC he was standing for the aedileship, and made his next big political splash by prosecuting Gaius Verres on a charge of provincial extortion. He represents himself as champion of the oppressed provincials but also, paradoxically, of the Senate by claiming Verres' guilt was so notorious that an acquittal would be clear evidence of corruption on the part of senatorial *iudices* ('judges' or in our terms 'jurors'), and thus would justify the removal of control of the courts from the senatorial class. He thus adroitly avoids being tarred with the over-*popularis* brush which might have naturally been seen as colouring a *novus homo* attacking the corruption of a senator. (Pompey and Crassus weakened senatorial control of the courts anyway.)

Pompey used the revitalized tribunate to acquire extraordinary commands or transfers of command through tribunician laws, passed by an assembly of the people, in 67 and 66 BC. The first assigned him command against the pirates who were threatening Rome's corn-supply, with *imperium* over not only the fleet but also all the Mediterranean provinces up to fifty miles inland. Showing outstanding administrative as much as military ability, he wrapped up this assignment in a single year, ending up in the eastern Mediterranean where another war against Mithridates VI had been waged for several years by Lucius Licinius Lucullus (mentioned at *Mil.* 73). The transfer of command to Pompey by a tribunician law may have been reminiscent of what had happened in 88 BC, but Lucullus, unpopular with his troops and far away, was in no position to march on Rome. Conservatives in the Senate had argued unsuccessfully against both tribunician laws, so Pompey's position at this point seemed to be defined as *popularis* by the nature of his tactics and the identity of his opponents, with worrying overtones of Sulla to boot. In 66 BC Cicero, as praetor, gave what he says was his first speech to the *populus* in support of the transfer of command (the extant *De Imperio Gnaei Pompei*). Although he may have in some respects appeared to be acting in a *popularis* manner in this instance, he takes care to praise Lucullus and treat the opponents of the law with the greatest possible respect. As a *novus homo* he was going to need all the help he could get to gain the consulship; the chance of gaining the popular vote through support of the people's hero, Pompey, was presumably too good to miss, but he tried at least not to alienate the more conservative senatorial powers.

Cicero's consular canvass came in 64 BC, while Pompey was in the East. A handful of surviving letters show him considering every angle possible in his campaign. In 65 BC he considered defending a fellow-candidate, Catiline (Lucius Sergius Catilina, mentioned explicitly at *Mil.* 37, 64), against a charge of political extortion, despite believing him to be guilty, in the hope of striking a pact of mutual support. Compounding the irony is the fact that the prosecutor, said to be prepared to make a deal, was the young Clodius. These two men would subsequently be represented by Cicero as his greatest enemies. The details of Catiline's political programme will forever be obscured by the portrait Cicero was to paint of him. From a *nobilis* family, he was associated with plans for a general cancellation of debts, a prospect which always terrified the conservative elements at Rome. This may have been either a *popularis* move or primarily due to the substantial debts he himself is supposed to have acquired (not unusual in Roman politicians at an early stage of their career). The historian Sallust, no blind follower of Cicero, claims that Cicero achieved the consulship despite his status as a *novus homo* because the *nobiles* preferred a *novus homo* to the danger posed by Catiline, and fear of the latter's programme may have been an important factor in Cicero's success.

In his consular year, 63 BC, Cicero's time was taken up with a wide range of issues. In many of these, e.g. opposition to a tribunician land-reform bill and the defence of Gaius Rabirius when prosecuted for participation in a killing which took place under the auspices of the *s.c.u.*, Cicero took what has been seen as a conservative position, while still attempting to represent himself as a champion of the people (*popularis consul*). The combination may have been less inherently self-contradictory than has sometimes been assumed. With his non-*nobilis* background, he was always sensitive to the needs of at least the wealthy non-senatorial classes; if he can be said to have had a consistent policy through the twists and turns of the late 60s and

50s BC, it was a unity of all classes which he called *concordia ordinum*. However peculiarly Ciceronian this term may have been, it is plausible that he was not the only politician who thought conservative policies could be made to be, or represented as, 'popular'. His support of Pompey's Mithridatic command in 66 BC need not, therefore, be seen as a *popularis* stance betrayed by subsequent adoption of more conservative policies once he had achieved the consulship. He may have believed sincerely both that Pompey's extraordinary command was necessary to wrap up the war, and that revolutionary land-reform should be opposed.

His opposition to Catiline (referred to at *Mil.* 63, 82, 103) may not have been anti-*popularis* in its fundamentals; at some point – it is difficult to be certain exactly when, but probably after his second consular canvass in 63 BC was unsuccessful – Catiline went beyond *popularis* policies into something much closer to revolution. The extent of the 'Catilinarian conspiracy' is another unquantifiable, but he had some support among a few malcontent and possibly dissolute (would-be) politicians. At some point in October, Cicero managed to get the Senate sufficiently anxious to pass the *s.c.u.*, but carefully refrained from any intemperate action until he had hard evidence of revolutionary plans. This evidence came after Catiline himself left Rome in November, with reports coming in that he had joined troops raised among discontented veterans in Etruria. His supporters in the city attempted to gain the support of the ambassadors of a Gallic tribe, who instead turned informers and gave Cicero the opportunity to seize incriminating letters. Five men were arrested and compelled to admit their guilt. The question remained: what to do with them? The trial of Rabirius earlier in the year had raised questions over the legal scope of the *s.c.u.*; Cicero sought to avoid sole responsibility by holding a senatorial debate which ultimately led to a majority voting for summary execution. Alas for Cicero, this vote would not turn out to be enough to save him from being accused of, and made to suffer for, executing Roman citizens without trial.

At the end of the year one of the new tribunes (and an associate of Pompey), Metellus Nepos, attempted to prevent Cicero as out-going consul from addressing the people on the grounds that he had not allowed the accused conspirators to speak in their own defence. On this occasion Cicero turned the tables: limited to swearing the traditional oath that he had carried out his duties as consul, he swore instead that the state had been saved by his efforts alone. However anti-*popularis* his actions could be represented as being, at this stage he had succeeded in persuading the people that Catiline and his supporters had been sufficiently dangerous to merit such drastic treatment; his popularity intact for the moment, he was escorted home by the *populus* as a body as he had been on the night the conspirators were executed (cf. *Mil.* 73). Catiline's army was defeated in early 62 BC, and Rome now awaited, with trepidation, the return of the victorious Pompey. Cicero wrote to him, hoping to form a political alliance, but in emphasizing his own 'victory' over Catiline, he may have misjudged his addressee's tolerance of other successful politicians. Nevertheless reasonably friendly relations were maintained between the two men.

Instead Pompey had trouble with the Senate, some of whom will have held a grudge against him for his trampling over their will in 67 and 66 BC. He found it impossible to get the Senate to ratify his administrative arrangements in the East or his plans for settling his veteran soldiers. It may have been concluded, rightly, from his various actions that demonstrated a desire to operate within the constitution, that he would not act as a second Sulla, and that it was thus safe to defy him. But his frustration nevertheless drove him to drastic action. He formed a political pact with Crassus and Caesar (often referred to as 'the Three' or the 'first triumvirate' although unlike other triumvirates it had no official standing), both of whom were facing or anticipating similar frustration in relation to their own activities or policies. They appear to have asked Cicero to join them, but he refused, either because he had by now definitively thrown in his lot with the conservative senatorial element or because he genuinely believed that this pact, which went well beyond the mutual support in elections he had considered with Catiline, was unconstitutional. The pact was revealed early in Caesar's consulship (59 BC), when Pompey declared his support for Caesar's land-reform bill (confirming the *popularis* credentials of both), and Caesar pushed through Pompey's eastern settlement. Some elements in the Senate resisted strenuously; there was violence, and Caesar's consular colleague Bibulus eventually retired to his house and declared unfavourable omens for every single day, technically making any business that took place invalid. Cicero spoke against some of Caesar's actions, and thus perhaps incurred his enmity, but his principal nemesis was a younger man whose enmity had been established in 61 BC.

A *popularis* agitator and his opponent: Clodius and Milo

Publius Clodius Pulcher was of impeccable *nobilis* lineage, but may always have seen himself as a champion of the people, or chosen such an image either in order to gain power or as a form of personal rebellion. As with Catiline, the true character of the man is difficult to discern behind the clouds of Ciceronian invective. Around thirteen years younger than Pompey and Cicero, his first appearance on the historical stage sees him stirring up trouble among his brother-in-law Lucullus' troops in the Mithridatic war, an action perhaps already indicative of a character fond of living on the edge. Scandal clung to him, at least in Cicero's representation; he was accused of incest with at least one of his sisters (*Mil.* 73).

In December of 62 BC, in his early thirties, he was caught infiltrating the women-only religious festival of the Bona Dea ('Good Goddess') held in the house of the Pontifex Maximus, Julius Caesar. His motive was said to have been the desire to carry on an intrigue with Caesar's wife (*Mil.* 72–3, 86). There is some evidence that relations between Cicero and Clodius had been amicable up to this point, including the proposed collusion over the trial of Catiline in 65 BC. But at Clodius' trial for sacrilege in 61 BC, Cicero was in a position to break his alibi: Clodius claimed to have been out of Rome on the day of the festival, but Cicero testified to having seen him there. Although Clodius was acquitted due to massive bribery (*Mil.* 86), this testifying seems to have earned Cicero Clodius' undying hatred.

In 59 BC, Clodius announced his desire to hold the office of tribune of the plebs, probably attracted by its legislative powers. Unfortunately he was disqualified by his patrician ancestry. Clodius therefore proposed being adopted into a plebeian family. The adoptive father he put forward was younger than he was, making the procedure highly controversial and possibly illegal. Eventually Caesar, as Pontifex Maximus, sanctioned the adoption – according to Cicero, on the very day that he himself had spoken out against Caesar. Clodius had declared an extensive legislative programme, which included a law concerning those who had put Roman citizens to death without trial. It looked as if he was planning revenge on Cicero.

Clodius first passed a number of other laws which confirmed his *popularis* credentials but also tended to strengthen his own power-base, such as setting up a free grain dole and abolishing the existing restrictions on *collegia* (guilds/political associations), which he proceeded – at least in the account of his enemies – to deploy as street-gangs in order to ensure the passage of further laws through intimidation. Cicero represents these gangs as being crowded with slaves (*Mil.* 26, 36, 73). Clodius bought off the consuls of the year by passing a law assigning them lucrative provinces (probably referred to at *Mil.* 73). Pompey, who had assured Cicero of his support, was persuaded not to interfere. After the passing of the law under which he was threatened with prosecution, Cicero dithered for a while and received some signs of support from minor senators and the equestrian order, but eventually decided to go into voluntary exile in mid-March 58 BC, rather than face trial. He later represented this action as being taken in order to save the state from the violence that would have ensued from clashes between his supporters and those of Clodius (*Mil.* 36).

Clodius passed another law, specifically naming Cicero, forbidding him from approaching within 400 miles of Italy and confiscating his property. His house on the Palatine was destroyed (*Mil.* 87) and Clodius rendered it sacrosanct by having a shrine of Libertas constructed on the site; he was presenting himself as a champion of the *libertas* ('freedom') of the Roman people which had been trampled on by Cicero in the case of the Catilinarians. But in various other respects if not this one, he appears to have gone too far. No mere puppet of the powerful Three, who may all have supported the adoption which permitted him to run for tribune although it was Caesar who had carried it out, he pursued his own agenda even if it went against their wishes. Even before the year was out he was at loggerheads with Pompey over various issues, leading to rumours of him sending agents to assassinate the great man (*Mil.* 18–19). Finally he provoked Pompey to such an extent that the latter began to throw his weight behind the movement for Cicero's recall from exile.

This movement was supported by one of the consuls and most of the tribunes of 57 BC (*Mil.* 39), who included Publius Sestius and Titus Annius Milo (*Mil.* 94). The talents of this pair seem to have lain in the direction of organizing street-gangs of their own to counter those of Clodius (cf. *Mil.* 38); this is one of the few things we know about Milo, which tends to lead to a (perhaps unfair) characterization of the man as little but a thug. A *novus homo* from the Italian town of

Lanuvium (*Mil.* 27, 45-6), he is largely known to history because of his support of Cicero. As Clodius annoyed more and more people, such support may have seemed like an obvious move. Ultimately Pompey was to mobilize a coalition across the classes in support of Cicero's recall, which Cicero could proudly look upon as another example of *concordia ordinum* (*Mil.* 38, 39). Briefly perhaps, Milo could be seen to be on the side of Senate, people and Pompey (cf. *Mil.* 34, 68).

Cicero returned to Rome in late 57 BC, and proceeded to do battle with Clodius in various courts, and in the court of public opinion, over the rights and wrongs of his exile and associated events. In all these verbal battles, Cicero interprets his recall as meaning that his exile was wrong and that his treatment of the Catilinarians was therefore right (exile: *Mil.* 36; Catilinarians: *Mil.* 8, 36, 73, 83). Despite the shrine to Libertas, he successfully won back the site of his house; he also successfully defended Sestius when the latter was prosecuted on a charge of *vis* (violence). But defeat in the matter of Cicero's recall and these other points did not seem to hinder Clodius' career or his popularity; meanwhile Cicero, owing his recall to Pompey, lost his ability to speak out against the power of the Three and instead was compelled to speak for them. Relations among the Three themselves were becoming strained. Caesar was away in Gaul, gaining that military reputation which would eventually outstrip Pompey's, and Pompey and Crassus had never been good friends. In 56 BC (the year in which Clodius was aedile, thus escaping a prosecution by Milo; he himself brought an abortive prosecution against Milo which was repeatedly interrupted by outbreaks of violence; *Mil.* 40), the Three met up to settle their differences and reaffirm their pact; Pompey and Crassus then stood for a second joint consulship in 55 BC. Clodius supported Pompey's canvass, and the two men were reconciled (*Mil.* 21). It is unknown whether this had any substantial impact on Pompey's relations with Milo, who remained Clodius' inveterate enemy; it does not appear to have led to a break between Pompey and Cicero.

In 54 BC Crassus departed for the East, hoping to gain glory against the Parthians to equal that of his colleagues. Pompey took the governorship of Further Spain, but wielded that *imperium* at a distance, staying at Rome to keep an eye on things. Milo held the praetorship. Julia, Caesar's daughter and Pompey's wife, died in childbirth, destroying one of the bonds that held the two men together in spite of their mutual jealousy. There was so much violence at Rome that the elections to the magistracies could not be held; 53 BC began without any magistrates in office. News came of Crassus' defeat and ignominious death at the hands of the Parthians; there was no longer a third person to dilute any tensions between Pompey and Caesar. Pompey stepped in and organized the elections; according to Cicero, Clodius decided not to stand for praetor, although it was the first year he was qualified, because he would only be able to be in office for six months (*Mil.* 24). The consuls during this six months failed to hold the main elections – attempts to do so were interrupted by violence (*Mil.* 41) – with the result that 52 BC began, like 53 BC, without any magistrates other than the tribunes in office.

52 BC

This is the point at which begins the extraordinarily detailed narrative of the first century AD commentary-writer, Asconius. In many respects Asconius appears to have taken an approach to the material closer to that of a modern historian than an ancient one. He seems to have accumulated as much background information as possible in order to contextualize and explain the text of Cicero's speech, on which he was writing a commentary to assist his own sons in their reading of this great oratorical work. But it is dangerous to assume that because Asconius has no particular axe to grind, no grand narrative to construct – because he is not in fact writing what the ancients conceived of as 'history' at all – his account is straightforwardly and in every instance reliable. Although less sensationalizing than the accounts of Plutarch and Dio, and less obviously directed to a specific judicial/political goal than Cicero's speech itself, Asconius' work, written around a century after the events themselves, was dependent on the accounts of others, and most of those accounts will not have been neutral. His use of the senatorial records, or *Acta* (e.g. Asc. 31C), is frequently used to argue for his reliability, but there are two problems here: he does not always tell us that his information comes from this source; even when he does, it must be borne in mind that we do not know where the information in the *Acta* came from. On Asconius' own evidence the city in 52 BC was alive with rumours and contradictory accounts; who decided which events, statements and opinions were recorded, and how those things were worded? We should be particularly careful where Asconius purports to be telling us not only that such-and-such a thing happened, but why it happened and what the thoughts of those concerned were.

Asconius states that Milo was standing for the consulship, competing against two men who are known to have been adherents of Pompey, and that Clodius, who was standing for the praetorship, supported these men (Asc. 30–1C). Cicero is in agreement with this, although he puts the worst possible slant on Clodius' behaviour and avoids identifying Milo's competitors or their connections to Pompey (*Mil.* 25). But when Asconius tells us that part of Clodius' motivation was the knowledge that Milo as consul would rein in his activities as praetor, he is closely echoing Cicero, who had his own reasons for attributing this thought to Clodius (*Mil.* 25); we cannot know whether Asconius had additional evidence for this or whether he had simply come to the judgement that Cicero's claim was plausible in this case.

Similarly when Asconius tells us that Milo's *audacia* ('boldness', usually in a negative sense; not a quality Cicero would have admitted in Milo) was used on behalf of the 'better' sort (*melioribus partibus*), and that his canvass relied on the support of the 'good' (*bonorum studiis*), it is impossible to be sure that this is not also taken from Cicero or some other pro-Milonian source.

Asconius acknowledges that different sources give different dates for the skirmish between Milo and Clodius (18/17 January), showing that he did look at other intermediary sources beside the *Acta* and the *Pro Milone*. He gives both men's reasons for travelling, in opposite directions, on the *via Appia* that day, whereas Cicero only gives Milo's (*Mil.* 27; he eventually acknowledges that Clodius had been in Aricia, *Mil.* 51, but does not say why). The accounts of the retinues of both men match fairly closely (Asc. 31–2C; *Mil.* 28, 54–5), except that Cicero omits Milo's having two well-known gladiators in his train; when Asconius later weighs up the implications of each in terms of whether either man planned the encounter (Asc. 41C), his conclusion is more balanced than Cicero's but the argument that Clodius' retinue points to his being the ambusher is precisely that made by the orator (*Mil.* 54). At Asc. 31C he implies and at 41C he states explicitly that neither man planned an ambush; the neutrality of this statement is appealing, but not necessarily a sign of Asconius' independent access to 'the truth', which at the time was so hotly disputed. There had been at no point any independent investigation, nothing other than the highly emotive and partisan trials of the people involved, to establish the point beyond doubt. Asconius, and probably others before him, may have been deducing that the encounter was unplanned from the fact that each side accused the other of having planned it, with neither being able to make the claim stick.

In Asconius' account, after the retinues had begun to brawl, one of Milo's gladiators wounded Clodius with a spear, and the situation escalated. Clodius took refuge in an inn and Milo ordered him to be dragged out and finished off. Here again he attributes motive: Milo is said to have judged the situation to be dangerous enough even if he left Clodius alive, and that he would gain some satisfaction from having him killed (Asc. 31-2C). If Cicero's speech is the source for Clodius' unpleasant motivation, prosecution claims are probably the ultimate source for Milo's; it is unlikely that Milo or Cicero ever admitted such a calculation to have been made. This should be borne in mind when considering whether the *iudices* 'knew' that Cicero was lying, at least by omission, about the course of the encounter. Rather than 'knowing', they will have been choosing whether or not to believe the prosecution version of events, expressed in witness-statements or in orators' speeches.

The body of Clodius was brought back to Rome and displayed by his wife and adherents in order to rouse the crowd to fury. The next day it was cremated in the Senate-house, with predictable results (Asc. 32-3C; cf. *Mil.* 33, 61, 96.); the *Clodiani* then attacked the house of Lepidus, who held the position of *interrex* (an intermediary position put in place to allow elections to be held). According to Asconius, these actions caused the tide of opinion to turn against the *Clodiani*, which gave Milo the courage to return to the city; Cicero uses his willingness to return as a sign of his guilt-free conscience (*Mil.* 61, 62-3). The tribune Caelius, an associate of Cicero and Milo, held a *contio* (public meeting) at which Milo had the opportunity to give his side of the story (Asc. 33C). This meeting may have been no less rabble-rousing, although less literally incendiary, than the Clodian ones. At any rate street-violence continued until the Senate passed a version of the *s.c.u.* naming Pompey, who held proconsular *imperium*, as the person who should protect the state (Asc. 34C, *Mil.* 70). Order was restored, friends of Clodius and Milo made moves preparatory to legal action, and the events were debated in the Senate.

Only later was Pompey appointed consul without a colleague; Asconius says this move was proposed by Caesar's former consular colleague Bibulus, who had tried in vain to oppose the power of the Three in 59 BC (Asc. 35–6C). He says little about the motives of those who opted for this rather than the dictatorship – only that the *optimates* thought this course of action 'safer' (*tutius*) – and does not discuss Pompey's feelings at all. Whether he would have preferred the dictatorship or not, it seems likely that Pompey got considerable satisfaction out of such an extraordinary position being proposed for him by a man who had opposed him so bitterly in the past. It is possible that the conservative senators were already looking to woo him away from Caesar with such awards, or rather to widen already visible cracks in the relationship of the two men. But this is part of the bigger historical narrative, and Asconius does not discuss it. He notes signs of less-than-positive relations between Pompey and Milo (Asc. 35C, 36C; cf. *Mil.* 67, 66), then goes on to give details of various accusations made against Milo which do not make it into Cicero's speech (Asc. 37–8C). One interesting statement he makes seems to praise Cicero's courage and loyalty to his friend, which Asconius believes brought him much enmity including from Pompey himself (Asc. 38C). Asconius therefore presents a situation in which the odds look very much against Milo.

The details of Pompey's legislation are scattered through the narrative of preparations for the trial of Milo (Asc. 36C, 38C, 39C). A new law on *vis* was passed in the Senate, specifically mentioning three events: the skirmish in which Clodius was killed, the burning of the Senate-house, and the attack on Lepidus' house (*Mil.* 13). The law specified a new procedure for the trials: in the past the prosecution and defence speeches had always preceded the interrogation of witnesses, but now this order was to be reversed. The orators would not have the opportunity to ply their persuasive techniques until after three days of witness-statements; their speeches were also strictly time-limited, with two hours allotted to the prosecution and three to the defence. New instructions were also given for the selection of *iudices*, and Pompey instituted a new panel from whom these men were to be selected, by lot and by rejection from each side, after the witness-statements. The prosecution-witnesses painted Clodius' death in lurid and pathetic colours, rousing the watching crowd to fury; on the first day at least one of the defence-speakers, Marcellus, claimed to be frightened for his life. After this Pompey came into the forum with his soldiers and the peace was kept for two more days of witnesses. They were cross-examined by Cicero, Milo and Marcellus, but Asconius says nothing about whether or not these defence-speakers were able to make any inroads on their claims (Asc. 40C).

We come now to some of the most controversial aspects of the trial (Asc. 41–2C): the reasons for Cicero's poor performance, the relationship between the delivered and published versions of the speech, and the content of the former. Cicero published texts of many of his speeches, and in most cases the relationship between delivered and published versions is difficult to ascertain; we cannot be sure exactly when or under what circumstances he circulated his text of the *Pro Milone*. Plutarch and Dio say that Cicero was so terrified of Pompey's soldiers that he hardly managed to utter a word. If it is true that it was the defence who requested protection (and there is a letter of Cicero which seems to back that up), this seems unlikely. Asconius says rather that he was repeatedly interrupted by the shouting of the *Clodiani*. He also states that some version of what Cicero actually said survived until his day (*manet*), which is backed up by remarks and quotations in Quintilian and in another ancient commentator preserved in a medieval manuscript. This suggests that Cicero managed to say something at least. Scholars, however, have been divided on the question of what this 'other *Pro Milone*' might have been like, or where it came from; there is a debate, for example, as to whether shorthand techniques had been sufficiently developed by this time for the speech to be taken down as it was delivered. Asconius tells us that there was disagreement in Milo's camp as to the line of defence that could be taken, although he may be extrapolating from the fact that Brutus, Caesar's future assassin, published a pamphlet in the form of a defence-speech (also known to Quintilian) which relied purely on the claim that the death of Clodius was in the best interests of Rome. When he attributes Cicero's disagreement with this tactic to a belief that 'a man [should not] be executed without being first sentenced', this is no more than any intelligent person might deduce about the man who had been attacked for his part in the execution of the Catilinarians.

Asconius had stated earlier that Milo and Caelius, in a *contio* shortly after the former's return to Rome, had already accused Clodius of ambushing Milo (Asc. 33C); he now states that Cicero got the idea for this argument from the equally false, opposite argument of the prosecution. Is he simply writing carelessly, or does he think that the prosecution had already made claims about an ambush in their incendiary speeches before Milo's return and Clodius' *contio*, and that was when there was a disagreement in Milo's camp as to which was the best defence-line to take? Or is he focusing on the mutual incompatibility of the claims in order to underline his own assertion that the encounter was planned by neither man? He then says that Cicero's whole speech *spectavit* ('kept in view') the ambush-argument. This statement has been used in support of the claim that the last third or so of our extant text, which is closer to Brutus' argument, was not part of the delivered speech. But the word *spectavit* is worth noting; it is noteworthy that Cicero's version of the 'best interests of the state' argument is presented as a counterfactual conditional: '*if* he had killed Clodius for the sake of the state [i.e. he did not], he ought to be rewarded rather than punished.' This argument never in fact loses sight of the claim that Clodius ambushed Milo. None of the other evidence tells us much about the content of the delivered speech: for Plutarch and Dio, it barely exists; Quintilian says only that he digressed in the *exordium* ('introduction'), as he does in the published speech.

Asconius' only remark about the published version, the one he is commenting on, can be read two ways: 'he wrote [it] with such wonderful artistry (*ita perfecte*) that it could quite reasonably be considered first (*haberi prima*)'. Does he mean that it was such a well-composed speech that it can be ranked as Cicero's best, or that it was written in such a convincing way that it could be taken for the original, i.e. the delivered version? Quintilian obviously rated the *Pro Milone* very highly, citing it frequently and praising it explicitly; Dio has an anecdote in which Milo offers it a (perhaps somewhat backhanded) compliment. (On receiving his copy in exile, he said that he would not be enjoying the renowned Massilian seafood if it had been delivered.) But the fact that others thought well of the speech does not settle the question of what Asconius means by *prima*. Unfortunately neither interpretation really tells us much. By this stage in his career Cicero will have been more than capable of writing something that read like a speech, whether it was delivered or not; other texts in the canon either may not have been or definitely were not delivered, specifically the five speeches from the prosecution of Verres and the attack on Marc Antony known as the second *Philippic*. Asconius' positive evaluation is no surprise, then, and it tells us nothing about the content of the two versions. Once again, having more evidence does not necessarily lead us to certainty, and perhaps the whole affair would be less intriguing if it did. We can still come to our own conclusions.

After some explanatory notes on the text itself, Asconius wraps up his commentary by giving us precise details of the *iudices*' votes and attributing the negative verdict to the belief that Milo had ordered Clodius' death. Given that he could not go back in time to interview all fifty-one *iudices*, and that it is unlikely that any contemporary did so, this can only be a guess, and it ties in with Asconius' own narrative. He then tells us that Milo was also convicted *in absentia* on a charge of electoral corruption, and again under another law on *vis*, and goes on to give details of some other trials that followed. He says that most of those convicted were *Clodiani*, and we know from Cicero's letters in December that he gained some considerable satisfaction from the conviction of one in particular, Plancus Bursa, who had worked so hard to rouse the people against Milo (Asc. 32–3C, 37–8C, 40C; *Mil.* 3, 45).

The speech

The structure of the *Pro Milone* is extremely clear and can be summarized as follows:

1. §§1–6   *exordium* ('introduction').
2. §§7–23   preliminary arguments:

   ○ self-defence is a valid justification for killing an attacker
   ○ the Senate have not already condemned Milo
   ○ Pompey has not already condemned Milo.

3. §§24–31   *narratio* ('statement of facts').
4. §§32–66   principal argument: Milo acted in self-defence.
5. §§67–71   transition.
6. §§72–91   supplementary argument: Clodius' death was in the best interests of the state; even if Milo had not acted in self-defence, he should be rewarded rather than punished.
7. §§92–105 *peroratio* ('closing statement').

The *exordium*, *narratio* and *peroratio* are particularly clearly marked, and the correspondence between the *narratio* and part of the principal argument is very close, with §§24–6/32–43 dealing with the period before the skirmish and §§27–9/44–56 with the skirmish itself; §§57–66 then deal with the period after the skirmish, which the *narratio* does not cover. The sections dealing with the period before the skirmish and the skirmish itself can be broken down still further into individual topics, e.g.:

- Clodius' motive for killing Milo: §25, §32.
- Clodius' opposition aided Milo's consular candidacy: §26, §34.
- Clodius' knowledge of Milo's movements: §27, §45.
- Contrast between Clodius' and Milo's retinues: §28, §§54–5.

At some points the correspondence stretches to the repetition of groups of words, e.g.:

1. §26 quin etiam **Marco Favonio,** fortissimo viro, quaerenti ex eo qua spe fureret Milone vivo, respondit **triduo illum** aut summum quadriduo **esse periturum.**
2. §44 vos ex **Marco Favonio** audistis Clodium sibi dixisse, et audistis vivo Clodio, **periturum Milonem triduo.**
3. §27 . . . ut **contionem** turbulentam in qua eius furor desideratus est, quae illo ipso die habita est, relinqueret, **quam, nisi** obire **facinoris** locum tempusque voluisset, **numquam reliquisset.**
4. §45 quo, ut ante dixi, fuit insanissima contio ab ipsius mercennario tribuno plebis concitata: quem diem ille, **quam contionem,** quos clamores, **nisi** ad cogitatum **facinus** approperaret, **numquam reliquisset.**
5. §28 obviam fit ei Clodius, expeditus, **in equo,** nulla **raeda,** nullis impedimentis, nullis **Graecis comitibus,** ut solebat, **sine uxore,** quod **numquam** fere.
6. §55 semper ille antea cum **uxore,** tum **sine** ea; **numquam** nisi in **raeda,** tum **in equo; comites Graeculi,** quocumque ibat, etiam cum in castra Etrusca properabat, tum nugarum in comitatu nihil.

The clarity of the structure raises the question of the speech's adherence to the 'rules' laid down in the rhetorical handbooks.

The ability to speak persuasively in public was extremely important in ancient Rome, where a relatively small proportion of the population would have been able to read. This was also true in Greece, where in the fifth century BC the techniques of speaking began to be analysed and codified as the art/science of rhetoric. By the first century BC, the Romans had inherited the systems and the disagreements of the Greek rhetoricians, which circulated in lectures and in teaching texts known as 'rhetorical handbooks'. As a young man Cicero had published such a handbook, the *De Inventione*; in the 50s BC, however, he would repudiate this work as derivative and limited, attempting to develop instead a more sophisticated, less rule-bound and most especially Roman analysis of public speaking. At the same period, he appears in many of his speeches to be moving away from the standard organization of his speeches according to the *partes orationis* ('parts of the speech') sequence of the rhetoricians: *exordium–narratio–*argument*–peroratio*. The rhetoricians divided the argument into *confirmatio* ('assertion', i.e. arguments supporting one's own case) and *confutatio* ('denial', i.e. those refuting the opposition's case), but this is seldom an important structural principle in any of Cicero's speeches. Stripped of these disputed cases, the *partes orationis* sequence may seem little more than common sense, especially the recommendation of an introduction and a conclusion. But the Ciceronian speeches closest in date to the *Pro Milone*, the defences of Sestius and Caelius in 56 BC, do not employ the clear-cut *narratio*-argument sequence; this can be taken as another sign, in addition to Cicero's explicit statements, that he was moving away from close adherence to the old handbooks. A speech relating to a trial in 52 BC, which corresponds to the sequence, therefore demands some explanation.

In this respect the *Pro Milone* resembles nothing so much as Cicero's first public case, the defence of Sex. Roscius in 80 BC. There are several possible explanations for this. Cicero may have been trying to exploit the rhetorical education that many of the *iudices* would have had, shaping his speech to the standard structure and standard arguments in order to give it a sense of familiarity and 'right-ness' that might to some extent make up, psychologically, for the obvious problems in the defence-case. Alternatively, if these features are seen as belonging to the published version, he may have deliberately set out to create a speech whose conformity to the 'rules' would make it popular with the teachers looking for oratorical texts to teach in schools, which might ensure that his definitive summary of Clodius' career would continue to be read. Or the conformity with the rhetorical rules could be more of a coincidence, arising from the nature of the case itself: the fact that a single incident was at issue, rather than the nebulous collection of on-going activities which were the focus of the *vis*-trials of Sestius and Caelius. Although Milo was also tried on a charge of *vis*, not murder, the trial seems to have played out like a murder-trial, like that of Roscius.

The handbooks recommend building your arguments on the *narratio* you have already delivered, as Cicero does in the *Pro Milone*, but this too can be seen simply as common sense. It has also been noted that many of the standard arguments from probability to be found in the handbooks are trotted out by Cicero in the principal argument (Clodius had a motive, he had means, he had opportunity), whereas there are many speeches in which they do not appear; again this could be explained either by the fact that the case was focused on a single incident, about which such arguments could more easily be constructed, or by the theory that hitting all the familiar notes from the handbooks was supposed to provide the *iudices* with some kind of reassurance about the argument. And the two explanations are not mutually exclusive; Cicero may have had more than one reason for his decisions about what to include and how to structure it.

Finally it should be noted that the rhetorical handbook issue cannot help us with the question of the relationship between the delivered and published versions of Milo's defence. The more detailed rhetorical handbooks acknowledged the possibility of including a *digressio* among the *partes orationis*, so even if the supplementary argument is seen as digression from the principal argument, it need not disturb the audience's impression that the speech conforms to the handbook 'rules'. It is also important, as argued above, that the supplementary argument is expressed in a series of counterfactual conditionals which imply that Milo did not kill Clodius for the sake of the state, but in self-defence as claimed in the principal argument:

1. §72 de qua **si iam nollem** ita diluere crimen ut dilui, **tamen** impune Miloni palam clamare ac mentiri gloriose **liceret:** ...
2. §77 quam ob rem **si cruentum gladium tenens clamaret T. Annius:** '...', **esset uero timendum** quonam modo id ferret ciuitas?
3. §80 **confiteretur, confiteretur, inquam, si fecisset**, et magno animo et libenter, se fecisse, libertatis omnium causa, quod esset non confitendum modo sed etiam uere praedicandum.

At one point in the supplementary argument, Cicero even claims that the death of Clodius was the result of a divine plan. But even this hyperbolic suggestion recapitulates the self-defence argument, claiming that it was the gods who put it in Clodius' mind to ambush Milo, and thus brought about his destruction (§§84, 88). These reminders of the self-defence argument make it possible to describe the published text in the same terms as Asconius describes the delivered speech: it always keeps in view (*spectavit*) the claim that Clodius ambushed Milo.

Style and syntax

Style is a complex and difficult thing to analyse. The word itself has several different possible connotations. It can be used positively or negatively. It is used to refer to the form of a statement rather than its content, but style would not matter at all if form did not affect the understanding of content, i.e. the two are not so easily separable. Sometimes specific 'styles' are identified in an attempt to classify texts as belonging to one or another: the rhetorical handbooks talk of 'high', 'middle' and 'low' style, leading to endless debates about what features belong to each one. In practice, the study of style often seems to come down to merely the identification of specific linguistic features that correspond to a particular set of definitions. But it is not the ability to memorize a list of technical terms and their meanings, and then apply them to a text, which makes a good understanding of style, although this mechanical process is perhaps a helpful starting point. Rather, it is important to consider why we are singling out particular linguistic features for comment. Many of them have no intrinsic meaning. But they may contribute to the pleasing qualities of a text, or to its emotional effects.

One important aspect to consider in evaluating the effect of a particular stylistic choice is the extent to which it makes a phrase stand out from its surroundings. Once you have learned what alliteration is, for example, what is there to say about a particular example of it that you come across in your reading? You will have a better answer to this if you look around that example at its context. If it is the only alliterative phrase on the page, you may feel that this stylistic feature makes it stand out, and you can then go on to consider whether Cicero could have had any reason for wanting it to stand out. If on the other hand the page is crammed with alliteration, you can either decide that this is just something Cicero does all the time, or, if you look at some other pages and find this is not the case, you can consider whether the accumulation of alliterative effects on the first page makes a whole passage stand out, and return to the question of whether there could be any reason for this. It is also worth checking for other noteworthy stylistic features (or 'figures of speech') in the same place, because if Cicero has decided that a passage is worth emphasizing, he will probably not restrict himself to just one way of marking it. Is it a passage of high emotion? an argument of particular importance? something that he wants the *iudices* to remember?

There are also degrees of alliteration (and this applies to many figures of speech). Is only one letter being repeated in this phrase, or are there several alternating? How many repetitions are there? We often notice alliteration when the first letter is the same in several words – and some definitions of the term will insist that alliteration must involve first letters, but unfortunately even something as small as this can be disputed – but check whether the letter appears in the middle of words as well. All this will complicate your conclusion about whether any individual alliteration 'stands out': for example, you may find that three words beginning with the same letter constitute a reasonably common phenomenon, but that a sequence of six words beginning with the same letter makes you look again for a potential motivation. But you should not be afraid to state that you can see no particular motivation for something like an alliterative phrase. Sometimes Cicero simply likes to decorate his language with these flourishes; by this stage in his career, it was probably second nature.

Syntax is often thought of as separate from style, but it can also be treated as part of it. Cicero's sentences are sometimes horrifyingly complex to a non-native speaker of Latin, but this complexity probably had some kind of effect on a native speaker as well. Perhaps a complex sentence was designed to make the listener pay more attention; perhaps it reflected a particularly convoluted thought; perhaps Cicero had something to hide under all those subordinate clauses that do not seem to get very far. It seems likely that variation was important: a speech made up of identically-structured sentences could quickly get boring. As with other stylistic features, look out for concentrations of particular types of sentence: is there any pattern to where Cicero uses a series of simple statements, or a series of complex ones, or an ever-changing alternation? How does he ring the changes on the relationship of principal and subordinate clauses: principal clause preceding subordinate(s), following, or embedded within?

Certain features of Latin syntax seem specifically designed to make things difficult for the learner. Some of these are simply the result of the differences in the structure of the language between Latin and English, or of tendencies in historical development; others may be habits of a particular author or specifically chosen to draw attention to a certain part of the sentence. A key feature of elaborate Latin (a category to which Cicero's speeches definitely belong) is what is known as 'periodicity' or the 'periodic style': a tendency to make the listener wait for some element that will make sense of the rest of the sentence. The infamous tendency for the verb to drift to the end of its clause or sentence is one of the most obvious ways of achieving periodicity (although it is in fact far from universal), but there are many others, including the separation of nouns and adjectives in agreement, or on a larger scale, allowing one clause to interrupt another.

Watch out for the following.

- The use of the relative pronoun (or adjective) at the beginning of a sentence, or sometimes at the beginning of a group of clauses in the middle of a sentence, where 'who/which' does not work in English; this is known as the 'connecting relative', and can often b translated with 'and' or 'but' and a pronoun ('he', 'it', 'that'); especially in the phrase *quam ob rem*. E.g. *qu vitam suam* . . . , §56.

- Multiple connecting words at the beginning of a sentence, or at the beginning of a group of clauses in the middle of a sentence, indicating that one clause has barely started before another one interrupts it. E.g. *quam, nisi obire facinoris locum tempusque uoluisset*, §27; *ne quod ne suspicari quidem potuerim . . .* , §47. But be careful if the first connecting word is a relative; it may be a connecting relative. E.g. *Quos nisi manu misisset*, §58.
- A similar phenomenon, in which the connecting word introducing a subordinate clause comes immediately after the first word or phrase belonging to the clause being interrupted. E.g. *Seruos agrestis et barbaros, quibus siluas publicas depopulatus erat . . .* , §26.
- Places where the word or phrase before the connecting word belongs equally to both the interrupted and to the interrupting clause. E.g. *Publius Clodius, cum statuisset . . .* , *subito reliquit annum suum*, §24; cf. perhaps: *Haec sicuti exposui ita gesta sunt, iudices*, §30 – here *haec* may stand both as the nominative subject of *gesta sunt* in the principal clause and as the accusative object of *exposui* in the interrupting subordinate clause.
- Words that indicate a particular kind of subordinate clause must follow, such as a result clause or a correlative. E.g. *quanto ille plura miscebat, . . .* , §25; *qui ita iudicia poenamque contempserat . . .* , §43.
- Verbs that could introduce an accusative–infinitive construction, i.e. verbs of saying, thinking, believing, etc., of possibility or necessity. E.g. *occurebat ei . . .* , §25.
- Contrariwise, accusatives that are not clearly objects or dependent on prepositions might have alerted native speakers instantly to the possibility that this was an accusative–infinitive construction, and have them waiting for the infinitive and the introductory verb. E.g. *Insidias factas esse*, §31.

The remainder of this section consists of a glossary of terms for stylistic features which have sometimes been called 'figures of speech', each with one or two illustrative examples from the speech. If you cannot remember the terms, bear in mind that it is in any case more important that you be able to discuss the possible effects of the features you observe in the text; look for an alternative way to describe what Cicero is doing.

alliteration/assonance: the repetition of sounds/letters, 'alliteration' generally being used for consonants and 'assonance' for vowels or whole syllables. E.g. *non multos menses*, §24. See also **homoioptoton**.

anaphora: the repetition of the same word at the start of several phrases, clauses or sentences. E.g. *nihil dico quid res publica consecuta sit, nihil quid vos, nihil quid omnes boni; nihil sane id prosit Miloni . . .* , §30.

apostrophe: direct address to a specific audience, especially an unexpected one. E.g. *Te, Quinte Petili, appello, optimum et fortissimum virum, . . .* , §44.

asyndeton: the omission of connecting words, possibly creating an effect of abruptness or speed. E.g. *convocabat tribus; se interponebat; Collinam novam dilectu perditissimorum civium conscribebat*, §25.

chiasmus: change of order when two or more elements are repeated, resulting in the ABBA pattern, e.g. adjective–noun–noun–adjective, or object–verb–verb–object; it can extend to ABCCBA and beyond, and can be used with phrases and clauses as well as with words. E.g. ***Milonis manu** caedem esse factam, **consilio** vero **maioris alicuius**, §47. Contrast **parallelism**.

clausulae: certain favoured rhythmical endings to a clause or sentence. You are not expected to be able to recognize these yourself, but they may sometimes be mentioned in the commentary.

ellipse: the omission of words which can be supplied from context; especially common with the verb *esse*, particularly in the periphrastic forms of the passive. E.g. *mancam ac debilem praeturam futuram suam*, §25; *si hic illi, . . . si ille huic, . . .* , §31.

exclamatio: an abrupt or emotional exclamation. E.g. *Legite testimonia testium vestrorum!* §46.

homoioptoton: the repetition of case endings in the same position in one word, phrase, clause or sentence after another. The use of homoioptoton in sequential words or phrases can be considered **alliteration/assonance.** E.g. *fortissimum virum, inimicissimum suum, certissimum consulem*, §25; *Id vero, iudices, etiam dubitandum et diutius cogitandum est?* §53.

isocolon: a sequence of phrases or clauses of roughly the same length. This might be used to underline the similarity between points, or to point up differences between them by contrast. E.g. *non servos, non arma, non vim*, §36.

parallelism: use of the same order when two or more elements are repeated; contrast **chiasmus.** E.g. *Ita et senatus rem, non hominem, notavit, et Pompeius de iure, non de facto, quaestionem tulit*, §31.

pleonasm: the use of more words than strictly necessary. No examples are given: you will find plenty. But Cicero is not just being verbose; he needs to get his point into the heads of the *iudices*, and repetition – as all teachers know – is a good way of doing this. Bear in mind too that there was often, and especially at the trial of Milo, a lot of noise in the forum while the orators were speaking. Pleonasm allowed members of the audience to miss the occasional word but still follow what the orators were saying.

polyptoton: the repetition of the same word in a different grammatical form. E.g. *quem diem ille, quam contionem, quos clamores . . .* , §45.

prosopopoeia: taking on the voice of someone (or something) else. The most striking example in the speech is §§72–5, where Cicero takes on the voice of Milo (although he may have slipped back into his own voice by the end of the long sentence), but there are many more examples of varying length, e.g. §48 where Cicero voices a possible statement of the prosecution.

rhetorical question: a question the point of which is not to ask for information, but something else. Inasmuch as none of Cicero's questions in the speech are intended to be answered, they might all be seen as not asking for information, but the true rhetorical question is used to produce an effect or even make a statement. The audience can readily supply the answer, but the fact that they have to do so involves them more closely in what is being said. E.g. *quis enim erat civium qui sibi solutam Publi Clodi praeturam sine maxime rerum novarum metu proponeret?* §34 – the obvious answer is 'nobody', so the question is the equivalent of saying 'nobody would'; *Quo tandem animo hoc tyrannum illum tulisse creditis?* §35 – the obvious answer is 'a very bad spirit', so the question is the equivalent of stating that Clodius must have taken this in a very bad spirit.

tricolon (crescendo/auctum): a sequence of three elements (words, phrases or clauses) of increasing length or importance. There are also examples of tricola where the length of the elements decreases, and of course there are tetracola (four elements) and so on, but the tricolon crescendo is a particularly common phenomenon. E.g. *nulla raeda, nullis impedimentis, nullis Graecis comitibus,* §28; *Adde casus; adde incertos exitus pugnarum Martemque communem, qui . . . ; adde inscitiam pransi, poti, oscitantis ducis, qui . . . ,* §56.

Further reading

Fotheringham, L.S., 'Essay on approach: reading style for substance', in *Persuasive Language in Cicero's Pro Milone. A close reading and commentary* (London 2013), 1–84. An introduction to the historical, rhetorical and stylistic study of the speech.

Hölkeskamp, K.-J., *Reconstructing the Roman Republic: An Ancient Political Culture and Modern Research* (Princeton, 2010). A stimulating and polemical essay on the 'democratic turn' in research on the Roman Republic, which also provides an introduction to major contributions by scholars writing in languages other than English.

Morstein-Marx, R., *Mass Oratory and Political Power in the Late Roman Republic* (Cambridge, 2004). An incisive analysis of the role of oratory in late Republican politics.

Powell, J., ed., *Logos. Rational argument in classical rhetoric* (London 2007). Contains two chapters on the *Pro Milone* by Jaap Wisse (on the speech's relationship to rhetorical theory) and Lynn Fotheringham (on Cicero's technique of combining arguments).

Powell, J., 'Cicero's style', in C. Steel, ed., *The Cambridge Companion to Cicero* (Cambridge, 2013), 41–72. An analysis of Cicero's stylistic choices across his writings, with many examples.

Powell, J. & Paterson, J., eds., *Cicero the Advocate* (Oxford 2004). Contains a range of chapters on various aspects of Cicero's judicial oratory. Particularly recommended are Powell & Paterson's Introduction, and Christopher Craig's chapter (on invective, especially in the *Pro Milone*).

Seager, R., *Pompey the Great*, second edn (London, 2002). A standard biography in English on Pompeius.

Steel, C., *The End of the Roman Republic, 146–44 B.C.: Conquest and Crisis* (Edinburgh, 2013). A narrative history of the period.

Tempest, K., *Cicero: Politics and Persuasion in Ancient Rome* (London, 2011). A good recent biography with a strong emphasis on oratory.

http://rhetoric.byu.edu/ The 'Silva Rhetoricae' site hosted at Brigham Young University; includes a descriptive index of rhetorical figures.

Textual Variants

The text in this edition is based on the Oxford Classical Text of A. C. Clark (1921), though it differs in a very small number of places. In particular, conventionally abbreviated proper names have been expanded, to assist any users who want to read sections aloud.

Some pupils and teachers may prefer to use the edition of F. H. Colson (1893, but still in print). They may wish to note the following significant variations between Colson and this edition. Apart from these, there are numerous minor differences of spelling, punctuation and word-order.

Colson	this edition
27. a Lanuvinis	*omitted*
29. ... impetum adversi, raedarium occidunt.	... impetum; adversi raedarium occidunt
30. feris	feris etiam beluis
31. ut scelere solvamur	tum nos scelere solvamur
35. ille erat ut ...	illi erat ut ...
46. cuius iam pridem ... Romae	*omitted*
49. Ecquid ...	quid ...
49. Atque ...	atqui ...
50.	*begins* noctu occidisset: insidioso et pleno latronum in loco occidisset.
51. devertit Clodius ad Albanum	devertit Clodius ad se in Albanum
52. praedictam	praedicatam
52. reditus	reditum
53. putarat	putabat

55. tamen mulier ...	ipse Clodius tamen mulier ...
56. Semper [ille]	semper ipse
59. De servis ... in Clodium	*omitted*
59. non quin	non quia non
75. est minitatus	est minatus
75. poposcerat	posceret
79. Nempe haec est quaestio de interitu P. Clodi	*omitted*
79. cernimus	cernamus
79. avocare	evocare
80. confiteretur, inquam ...	confiteretur, confiteretur, inquam ...

Text

24. Publius Clodius, cum statuisset omni scelere in praetura vexare rem publicam videretque ita tracta esse comitia anno superiore ut non multos menses praeturam gerere posset, qui non honoris gradum spectaret, ut ceteri, sed et Lucium Paulum conlegam effugere vellet, singulari virtute civem, et annum integrum ad dilacerandam rem publicam quaereret, subito reliquit annum suum seseque in proximum transtulit, non, ut fit, religione aliqua, sed ut haberet, quod ipse dicebat, ad praeturam gerendam, hoc est ad evertendam rem publicam, plenum annum atque integrum.

25. occurrebat ei mancam ac debilem praeturam futuram suam consule Milone; eum porro summo consensu populi Romani consulem fieri videbat. contulit se ad eius competitores, sed ita totam ut petitionem ipse solus etiam invitis illis gubernaret, tota ut comitia suis, ut dictitabat, umeris sustineret. convocabat tribus, se interponebat, Collinam novam dilectu perditissimorum civium conscribebat. quanto ille plura miscebat, tanto hic magis in dies convalescebat. ubi vidit homo ad omne facinus paratissimus fortissimum virum, inimicissimum suum, certissimum consulem, idque intellexit non solum sermonibus, sed etiam suffragiis populi Romani saepe esse declaratum, palam agere coepit et aperte dicere occidendum Milonem.

A S

26. servos agrestes et barbaros, quibus silvas publicas depopulatus erat Etruriamque vexarat, ex Appennino deduxerat, quos videbatis. res erat minime obscura. etenim dictitabat palam consulatum Miloni eripi non posse, vitam posse. significavit hoc saepe in senatu, dixit in contione; quin etiam Marco Favonio, fortissimo viro, quaerenti ex eo qua spe fureret Milone vivo, respondit triduo illum aut summum quadriduo esse periturum; quam vocem eius ad hunc Marcum Catonem statim Favonius detulit.

27. interim cum sciret Clodius – neque enim erat id difficile scire – iter sollemne, legitimum, necessarium ante diem tertiam et decimam Kalendas Februarias Miloni esse Lanuvium ad flaminem prodendum, quod erat dictator Lanuvi Milo, Roma subito ipse profectus pridie est ut ante suum fundum, quod re intellectum est, Miloni insidias conlocaret; atque ita profectus est ut contionem turbulentam in qua eius furor desideratus est, quae illo ipso die habita est, relinqueret, quam, nisi obire facinoris locum tempusque voluisset, numquam reliquisset.

28. Milo autem cum in senatu fuisset eo die quoad senatus est dimissus, domum venit, calceos et vestimenta mutavit, paulisper, dum se uxor, ut fit, comparat, commoratus est, dein profectus id temporis cum iam Clodius, si quidem eo die Romam venturus erat, redire potuisset. obviam fit ei Clodius, expeditus, in equo, nulla raeda, nullis impedimentis, nullis Graecis comitibus, ut solebat, sine uxore, quod numquam fere: cum hic insidiator, qui iter illud ad caedem faciendam apparasset, cum uxore veheretur in raeda, paenulatus, magno et impedito et muliebri ac delicato ancillarum puerorumque comitatu.

29. fit obviam Clodio ante fundum eius hora fere undecima, aut non multo secus. statim complures cum telis in hunc faciunt de loco superiore impetum; adversi raedarium occidunt. cum autem hic de raeda reiecta paenula desiluisset seque acri animo defenderet, illi qui erant cum Clodio gladiis eductis partim recurrere ad raedam ut a tergo Milonem adorirentur, partim, quod hunc iam interfectum putarent, caedere incipiunt eius servos qui post erant; ex quibus qui animo fideli in dominum et praesenti fuerunt, partim occisi sunt, partim, cum ad raedam pugnari viderent, domino succurrere prohiberentur, Milonem occisum et ex ipso Clodio audirent et re vera putarent, fecerunt id servi Milonis – dicam enim aperte non derivandi criminis causa, sed ut factum est – nec imperante nec sciente nec praesente domino, quod suos quisque servos in tali re facere voluisset.

30. haec sicuti exposui ita gesta sunt, iudices: insidiator superatus est, vi victa vis vel potius oppressa virtute audacia est. nihil dico quid res publica consecuta sit, nihil quid vos, nihil quid omnes boni: nihil sane id prosit Miloni, qui hoc fato natus est ut ne se quidem servare potuerit quin una rem publicam vosque servaret. si id iure fieri non potuit, nihil habeo quod defendam. sin hoc et ratio doctis et necessitas barbaris et mos gentibus et feris etiam beluis natura ipsa praescripsit, ut omnem semper vim quacumque ope possent a corpore, a capite, a vita sua propulsarent, non potestis hoc facinus improbum iudicare quin simul iudicetis omnibus qui in latrones inciderint aut illorum telis aut vestris sententiis esse pereundum.

31. quod si ita putasset, certe optabilius Miloni fuit dare iugulum Publio Clodio, non semel ab illo neque tum primum petitum, quam iugulari a vobis, quia se non iugulandum illi tradidisset. sin hoc nemo vestrum ita sentit, illud iam in iudicium venit, non occisusne sit, quod fatemur, sed iure an iniuria, quod multis in causis saepe quaesitum est. insidias factas esse constat, et id est quod senatus contra rem publicam factum iudicavit; ab utro factae sint incertum est. de hoc igitur latum est ut quaereretur. ita et senatus rem, non hominem notavit et Pompeius de iure, non de facto quaestionem tulit. num quid igitur aliud in iudicium venit nisi uter utri insidias fecerit? profecto nihil: si hic illi, ut ne sit impune; si ille huic, tum nos scelere solvamur.

32. quonam igitur pacto probari potest insidias Miloni fecisse Clodium? satis est in illa quidem tam audaci, tam nefaria belua docere, magnam ei causam, magnam spem in Milonis morte propositam, magnas utilitates fuisse. itaque illud Cassianum 'cui bono fuerit' in his personis valeat, etsi boni nullo emolumento impelluntur in fraudem, improbi saepe parvo. atqui Milone interfecto Clodius haec adsequebatur, non modo ut praetor esset non eo consule quo sceleris facere nihil posset sed etiam ut eis consulibus praetor esset quibus, si non adiuvantibus, at coniventibus certe speraret se posse eludere in illis suis cogitatis furoribus: cuius illi conatus, ut ipse ratiocinabatur, nec cuperent reprimere, si possent, cum tantum beneficium ei se debere arbitrarentur, et, si vellent, fortasse vix possent frangere hominis sceleratissimi conroboratam iam vetustate audaciam.

33. *Cicero rounds on a henchman of Clodius, accusing him of possessing documents which would reveal the terrifying programme of legislation Clodius intended to pass in his praetorship.*

34. audistis, iudices, quantum Clodi interfuerit occidi Milonem: convertite animos nunc vicissim ad Milonem. quid Milonis intererat interfici Clodium? quid erat cur Milo, non dicam admitteret, sed optaret? 'obstabat in spe consulatus Miloni Clodius.' at eo repugnante fiebat, immo vero eo fiebat magis, nec me suffragatore meliore utebatur quam Clodio. valebat apud vos, iudices, Milonis erga me remque publicam meritorum memoria, valebant preces et lacrimae nostrae, quibus ego tum vos mirifice moveri sentiebam, sed plus multo valebat periculorum impendentium timor. quis enim erat civium qui sibi solutam Publi Clodi praeturam sine maximo rerum novarum metu proponeret? solutam autem fore videbatis, nisi esset is consul qui eam auderet possetque constringere. eum Milonem unum esse cum sentiret universus populus Romanus, quis dubitaret suffragio suo se metu, periculo rem publicam liberare? at nunc, Clodio remoto, usitatis iam rebus enitendum est Miloni ut tueatur dignitatem suam; singularis illa et huic uni concessa gloria, quae cotidie augebatur frangendis furoribus Clodianis, iam Clodi morte cecidit. vos adepti estis ne quem civem metueretis; hic exercitationem virtutis, suffragationem consulatus, fontem perennem gloriae suae perdidit. itaque Milonis consulatus qui vivo Clodio labefactari non poterat mortuo denique temptari coeptus est. non modo igitur nihil prodest sed obest etiam Clodi mors Miloni.

35. 'at valuit odium, fecit iratus, fecit inimicus, fuit ultor iniuriae, punitor doloris sui.' quid? si haec non dico maiora fuerunt in Clodio quam in Milone, sed in illo maxima, nulla in hoc, quid vultis amplius? quid enim odisset Clodium Milo, segetem ac materiam suae gloriae, praeter hoc civile odium quo omnes improbos odimus? illi erat ut odisset primum defensorem salutis meae, deinde vexatorem furoris, domitorem armorum suorum, postremo etiam accusatorem suum; reus enim Milonis lege Plotia fuit Clodius quoad vixit. quo tandem animo hoc tyrannum illum tulisse creditis? quantum odium illius et in homine iniusto quam etiam iustum fuisse?

36–42. *Cicero argues that Clodius was by nature a man of violence, whereas Milo's character was quite the opposite. He gives numerous examples of occasions when Milo could have killed Clodius quite justifiably but asserts he would not have killed him on the Appian Way, in circumstances impossible to justify, and with impending elections.*

43. hunc igitur diem Campi speratum atque exoptatum sibi proponens Milo, cruentis manibus, scelus et facinus prae se ferens et confitens, ad illa augusta centuriarum auspicia veniebat? quam hoc

non credibile est in hoc, quam idem in Clodio non dubitandum, qui
se ipse interfecto Milone regnaturum putaret! quid? quod caput est
audaciae, iudices, quis ignorat maximam inlecebram esse peccandi
impunitatis spem? in utro igitur haec fuit? in Milone qui etiam nunc
reus est facti aut praeclari aut certe necessarii, an in Clodio qui ita
iudicia poenamque contempserat ut eum nihil delectaret quod aut
per naturam fas esset aut per leges liceret?

44. sed quid ego argumentor, quid plura disputo? te, Quinte Petili,
appello, optimum et fortissimum civem; te, Marce Cato, testor, quos
mihi divina quaedam sors dedit iudices. vos ex Marco Favonio audistis
Clodium sibi dixisse, et audistis vivo Clodio, periturum Milonem
triduo. post diem tertium gesta res est quam dixerat. cum ille non
dubitarit aperire quid cogitaret, vos potestis dubitare quid fecerit?

45. quem ad modum igitur eum dies non fefellit? dixi equidem
modo. dictatoris Lanuvini stata sacrificia nosse negoti nihil erat. vidit
necesse esse Miloni proficisci Lanuvium illo ipso quo est profectus
die; itaque antevertit. at quo die? quo, ut ante dixi, fuit insanissima
contio ab ipsius mercennario tribuno plebis concitata: quem diem
ille, quam contionem, quos clamores, nisi ad cogitatum facinus
approperaret, numquam reliquisset. ergo illi ne causa quidem itineris,
etiam causa manendi; Miloni manendi nulla facultas, exeundi
non causa solum sed etiam necessitas fuit. quid si, ut ille scivit
Milonem fore eo die in via, sic Clodium Milo ne suspicari quidem
potuit?

46. primum quaero qui id scire potuerit, quod vos idem in Clodio
quaerere non potestis; ut enim neminem alium nisi Titum Patinam,
familiarissimum suum, rogasset, scire potuit illo ipso die Lanuvi a
dictatore Milone prodi flaminem necesse esse; sed erant permulti alii
ex quibus id facillime scire posset: omnes scilicet Lanuvini. Milo de
Clodi reditu unde quaesivit? quaesierit sane – videte quid vobis largiar

– servum etiam, ut Quintus Arrius, amicus meus, dixit, corruperit. legite testimonia testium vestrorum. dixit Gaius Causinius Schola, Interamnanus, familiarissimus et idem comes Clodi, Publium Clodium illo die in Albano mansurum fuisse, sed subito ei esse nuntiatum Cyrum architectum esse mortuum, itaque repente Romam constituisse proficisci. dixit hoc item comes Publi Clodi, Gaius Clodius.

47. videte, iudices, quantae res his testimoniis sint confectae. primum certe liberatur Milo non eo consilio profectus esse ut insidiaretur in via Clodio: quippe, si ille obvius ei futurus omnino non erat. deinde – non enim video cur non meum quoque agam negotium – scitis, iudices, fuisse qui in hac rogatione suadenda dicerent Milonis manu caedem esse factam, consilio vero maioris alicuius. me videlicet latronem ac sicarium abiecti homines et perditi describebant. iacent suis testibus, qui Clodium negant eo die Romam, nisi de Cyro audisset, fuisse rediturum. respiravi, liberatus sum; non vereor ne, quod ne suspicari quidem potuerim, videar id cogitasse.

48. nunc persequar cetera; nam occurrit illud: 'igitur ne Clodius quidem de insidiis cogitavit, quoniam fuit in Albano mansurus' – si quidem exiturus ad caedem e villa non fuisset. video enim illum qui dicatur de Cyri morte nuntiasse non id nuntiasse, sed Milonem appropinquare. nam quid de Cyro nuntiaret, quem Clodius Roma proficiscens reliquerat morientem? una fui, testamentum simul obsignavi; testamentum autem palam fecerat et illum heredem et me scripserat. quem pridie hora tertia animam efflantem reliquisset, eum mortuum postridie hora decima denique ei nuntiabatur?

49. age, sit ita factum: quae causa fuit cur Romam properaret, cur in noctem se coniceret? quid adferebat festinationis quod heres erat? primum nihil erat cur properato opus esset; deinde si quid esset, quid tandem erat quod ea nocte consequi posset, amitteret autem, si postridie Romam mane venisset? atqui ut illi nocturnus ad urbem adventus vitandus potius quam expetendus fuit, sic Miloni, cum insidiator esset, si illum ad urbem noctu accessurum sciebat, subsidendum atque exspectandum fuit.

50. noctu occidisset: insidioso et pleno latronum in loco occidisset. nemo ei neganti non credidisset quem esse omnes salvum etiam confitentem volunt. sustinuisset crimen primum ipse ille latronum occultator et receptor locus, tum neque muta solitudo indicasset neque caeca nox ostendisset Milonem; deinde multi ab illo violati, spoliati, bonis expulsi, multi haec etiam timentes in suspicionem caderent, tota denique rea citaretur Etruria.

51. atque illo die certe Aricia rediens devertit Clodius ad se in Albanum. quod ut sciret Milo, illum Ariciae fuisse, suspicari tamen debuit eum, etiam si Romam illo die reverti vellet, ad villam suam quae viam tangeret deversurum. cur nec ante occurrit ne ille in villa resideret, nec eo in loco subsedit quo ille noctu venturus esset?

52. video adhuc constare, iudices, omnia: Miloni etiam utile fuisse Clodium vivere, illi ad ea quae concupierat optatissimum interitum Milonis; odium fuisse illius in hunc acerbissimum, nullum huius in illum; consuetudinem illius perpetuam in vi inferenda, huius tantum in repellenda; mortem ab illo Miloni denuntiatam et praedicatam palam, nihil umquam auditum ex Milone; profectionis huius diem illi notum, reditum illius huic ignotum fuisse; huius iter necessarium, illius etiam potius alienum; hunc prae se tulisse se illo die exiturum, illum eo die se dissimulasse rediturum; hunc nullius rei mutasse consilium, illum causam mutandi consili finxisse; huic, si insidiaretur, noctem prope urbem exspectandam, illi, etiam si hunc non timeret, tamen accessum ad urbem nocturnum fuisse metuendum.

53. videamus nunc id quod caput est, locus ad insidias ille ipse ubi congressi sunt utri tandem fuerit aptior. id vero, iudices, etiam dubitandum et diutius cogitandum est? ante fundum Clodi quo in fundo propter insanas illas substructiones facile hominum mille versabatur valentium, edito adversarii atque excelso loco superiorem se fore putabat Milo, et ob eam rem eum locum ad pugnam potissimum elegerat, an in eo loco est potius exspectatus ab eo qui ipsius loci spe facere impetum cogitarat? res loquitur ipsa, iudices, quae semper valet plurimum.

54. si haec non gesta audiretis, sed picta videretis, tamen appareret uter esset insidiator, uter nihil mali cogitaret, cum alter veheretur in raeda paenulatus, una sederet uxor. quid horum non impeditissimum, vestitus an vehiculum an comes? quid minus promptum ad pugnam, cum paenula inretitus, raeda impeditus, uxore paene constrictus esset? videte nunc illum, primum egredientem e villa, subito: cur? vesperi: quid necesse est? tarde: qui convenit, praesertim id temporis? 'devertit in villam Pompei.' Pompeium ut videret? sciebat in Alsiensi esse. villam ut perspiceret? miliens in ea fuerat. quid ergo erat? mora et tergiversatio: dum hic veniret, locum relinquere noluit.

55. age nunc; iter expediti latronis cum Milonis impedimentis comparate. semper ille antea cum uxore, tum sine ea; numquam nisi in raeda, tum in equo; comites Graeculi quocumque ibat, etiam cum in castra Etrusca properabat, tum nugarum in comitatu nihil. Milo, qui numquam, tum casu pueros symphoniacos uxoris ducebat et ancillarum greges. ille, qui semper secum scorta, semper exoletos, semper lupas duceret, tum neminem, nisi ut virum a viro lectum esse diceres. cur igitur victus est? quia non semper viator a latrone, nonnumquam etiam latro a viatore occiditur: quia, quamquam paratus in imparatos Clodius, ipse Clodius tamen mulier inciderat in viros.

56. nec vero sic erat umquam non paratus Milo contra illum ut non satis fere esset paratus. semper ipse et quantum interesset Publi Clodi se interire et quanto illi odio esset et quantum ille auderet cogitabat. quam ob rem vitam suam, quam maximis praemiis propositam et paene addictam sciebat, numquam in periculum sine praesidio et sine custodia proiciebat. adde casus, adde incertos exitus pugnarum Martemque communem, qui saepe spoliantem iam et exsultantem evertit et perculit ab abiecto; adde inscitiam pransi, poti, oscitantis ducis, qui, cum a tergo hostem interclusum reliquisset, nihil de eius extremis comitibus cogitavit, in quos incensos ira vitamque domini desperantes cum incidisset, haesit in eis poenis quas ab eo servi fideles pro domini vita expetiverunt.

57. cur igitur eos manu misit? metuebat scilicet ne indicaretur, ne dolorem perferre non possent, ne tormentis cogerentur occisum esse a servis Milonis in Appia Via Publium Clodium confiteri. quid opus est tortore? quid quaeris? occideritne? occidit. iure an iniuria? nihil ad tortorem: facti enim in eculeo quaestio est, iuris in iudicio. quod igitur in causa quaerendum est, id agamus hic; quod tormentis invenire vis, id fatemur. manu vero cur miserit, si id potius quaeris quam cur parum amplis adfecerit praemiis, nescis inimici factum reprehendere.

58. dixit enim hic idem, qui omnia semper constanter et fortiter, Marcus Cato, et dixit in turbulenta contione, quae tamen huius auctoritate placata est, non libertate solum, sed etiam omnibus praemiis dignissimos fuisse, qui domini caput defendissent. quod enim praemium satis magnum est tam benevolis, tam bonis, tam fidelibus servis, propter quos vivit? etsi id quidem non tanti est quam quod propter eosdem non sanguine et vulneribus suis crudelissimi inimici mentem oculosque satiavit. quos nisi manu misisset, tormentis etiam dedendi fuerunt conservatores domini, ultores sceleris, defensores necis. hic vero nihil habet in his malis quod minus moleste ferat quam, etiam si quid ipsi accidat, esse tamen illis meritum praemium persolutum.

59. sed quaestiones urgent Milonem, quae sunt habitae nunc in atrio Libertatis. 'quibusnam de servis?' rogas; de Publi Clodi. 'quis eos postulavit?' Appius. 'quis produxit?' Appius. 'unde?' ab Appio. di boni! quid potest agi severius? proxime deos accessit Clodius, propius quam tum cum ad ipsos penetrarat, cuius de morte tamquam de caerimoniis violatis quaeritur. sed tamen maiores nostri in dominum quaeri noluerunt, non quia non posset verum inveniri, sed quia videbatur indignum esse et dominis morte ipsa tristius. in reum de servo accusatoris cum quaeritur, verum inveniri potest?

60. age vero, quae erat aut qualis quaestio? 'heus tu, Rufio,' (verbi causa) 'cave sis mentiare. Clodius insidias fecit Miloni?' 'fecit.' certa crux. 'nullas fecit.' sperata libertas. quid hac quaestione certius? subito adrepti in quaestionem, tamen separantur ceteri et in arcas coniciuntur, ne quis cum eis conloqui possit. hi centum dies penes accusatorem cum fuissent, ab eo ipso accusatore producti sunt. quid hac quaestione dici potest integrius, quid incorruptius?

61. quod si nondum satis cernitis, cum res ipsa tot tam claris argumentis signisque luceat, pura mente atque integra Milonem, nullo scelere imbutum, nullo metu perterritum, nulla conscientia exanimatum, Romam revertisse, recordamini (per deos immortales!) quae fuerit celeritas reditus eius, qui ingressus in forum ardente curia, quae magnitudo animi, qui vultus, quae oratio. neque vero se populo solum, sed etiam senatui commisit; neque senatui modo, sed etiam publicis praesidiis et armis; neque his tantum, verum etiam eius potestati cui senatus totam rem publicam, omnem Italiae pubem, cuncta populi Romani arma commiserat: cui numquam se hic profecto tradidisset, nisi causae suae confideret, praesertim omnia audienti, magna metuenti, multa suspicanti, nonnulla credenti. magna

A
Level

vis est conscientiae, iudices, et magna in utramque partem, ut neque timeant qui nihil commiserint, et poenam semper ante oculos versari putent qui peccarint.

62. neque vero sine ratione certa causa Milonis semper a senatu probata est. videbant enim sapientissimi homines facti rationem, praesentiam animi, defensionis constantiam. an vero obliti estis, iudices, recenti illo nuntio necis Clodianae, non modo inimicorum Milonis sermones et opiniones, sed nonnullorum etiam imperitorum? negabant eum Romam esse rediturum.

63. sive enim illud animo irato ac percito fecisset, ut incensus odio trucidaret inimicum, arbitrabantur eum tanti mortem Publi Clodi putasse ut aequo animo patria careret, cum sanguine inimici explesset odium suum; sive etiam illius morte patriam liberare voluisset, non dubitaturum fortem virum quin, cum suo periculo salutem populo Romano attulisset, cederet aequo animo legibus, secum auferret gloriam sempiternam, vobis haec fruenda relinqueret quae ipse servasset. multi etiam Catilinam atque illa portenta loquebantur: 'erumpet, occupabit aliquem locum, bellum patriae faciet.' miseros interdum cives optime de re publica meritos, in quibus homines non modo res praeclarissimas obliviscuntur sed etiam nefarias suspicantur!

64. ergo illa falsa fuerunt, quae certe vera exstitissent, si Milo admisisset aliquid quod non posset honeste vereque defendere ...

64–71. *Cicero refers to a number of wild accusations made against Milo – that he had stashed weapons away in secret places and even planned to assassinate Pompey. He praises both Milo and Pompey for their careful responses to these rumours, which were investigated and found groundless.*

72. nec vero me, iudices, Clodianum crimen movet, nec tam sum demens tamque vestri sensus ignarus atque expers, ut nesciam quid de morte Clodi sentiatis. de qua, si iam nollem ita diluere crimen ut dilui, tamen impune Miloni palam clamare ac mentiri gloriose liceret: 'occidi, occidi, non Spurium Maelium, qui annona levanda iacturisque rei familiaris, quia nimis amplecti plebem videbatur, in suspicionem incidit regni appetendi; non Tiberium Gracchum, qui conlegae magistratum per seditionem abrogavit, quorum interfectores impleverunt orbem terrarum nominis sui gloria; sed eum' – auderet enim dicere, cum patriam periculo suo liberasset – 'cuius nefandum adulterium in pulvinaribus sanctissimis nobilissimae feminae comprehenderunt.

73. 'eum cuius supplicio senatus sollemnes religiones expiandas saepe censuit; eum quem cum sorore germana nefarium stuprum fecisse Lucius Lucullus iuratus se quaestionibus habitis dixit comperisse; eum qui civem quem senatus, quem populus Romanus, quem omnes gentes urbis ac vitae civium conservatorem iudicarant servorum armis exterminavit; eum qui regna dedit, ademit, orbem terrarum quibuscum voluit partitus est; eum qui, plurimis caedibus in foro factis, singulari virtute et gloria civem domum vi et armis compulit; eum cui nihil umquam nefas fuit, nec in facinore nec in libidine; eum qui aedem Nympharum incendit, ut memoriam publicam recensionis tabulis publicis impressam exstingueret;

74. 'eum denique, cui iam nulla lex erat, nullum civile ius, nulli possessionum termini; qui non calumnia litium, non iniustis vindiciis ac sacramentis alienos fundos, sed castris, exercitu, signis inferendis petebat; qui non solum Etruscos – eos enim penitus contempserat – sed hunc Publium Varium, fortissimum atque optimum civem, iudicem nostrum, pellere possessionibus armis castrisque conatus est; qui cum architectis et decempedis villas multorum hortosque peragrabat; qui Ianiculo et Alpibus spem possessionum terminarat suarum; qui, cum ab equite Romano splendido et forti, Marco Paconio, non impetrasset ut sibi insulam in lacu Prilio venderet, repente lintribus in eam insulam materiem, calcem, caementa, harenam convexit, dominoque trans ripam inspectante non dubitavit aedificium exstruere in alieno;

75. 'qui huic Tito Furfanio – cui viro, di immortales! quid enim ego de muliercula Scantia, quid de adulescente Publio Aponio dicam? quorum utrique mortem est minatus nisi sibi hortorum possessione cessissent – sed ausum esse Tito Furfanio dicere, si sibi pecuniam quantam posceret non dedisset, mortuum se in domum eius inlaturum, qua invidia huic esset tali viro conflagrandum; qui Appium fratrem, hominem mihi coniunctum fidissima gratia, absentem de possessione fundi deiecit; qui parietem sic per vestibulum sororis instituit ducere, sic agere fundamenta, ut sororem non modo vestibulo privaret, sed omni aditu et limine.'

76. quamquam haec quidem iam tolerabilia videbantur (etsi aequabiliter in rem publicam, in privatos, in longinquos, in propinquos, in alienos, in suos inruebat, sed nescioquo modo iam usu obduruerat et percalluerat civitatis incredibilis patientia), quae vero aderant iam et impendebant, quonam modo ea aut depellere potuissetis aut ferre? imperium ille si nactus esset – omitto socios, exteras nationes, reges, tetrarchas; vota enim faceretis ut in eos se potius immitteret quam in vestras possessiones, vestra tecta, vestras pecunias: pecunias dico? a liberis (me dius fidius!) et a coniugibus vestris numquam ille effrenatas suas libidines cohibuisset. fingi haec putatis, quae patent, quae nota sunt omnibus, quae tenentur, servorum exercitus illum in urbe conscripturum fuisse, per quos totam rem publicam resque privatas omnium possideret?

77. quam ob rem si cruentum gladium tenens clamaret Titus Annius, 'Adeste, quaeso, atque audite, cives: Publium Clodium interfeci; eius furores, quos nullis iam legibus, nullis iudiciis frenare poteramus, hoc ferro et hac dextera a cervicibus vestris reppuli, per me ut unum ius, aequitas, leges, libertas, pudor, pudicitia in civitate maneret,' esset vero timendum quonam modo id ferret civitas? nunc enim quis est qui non probet, qui non laudet, qui non unum post hominum memoriam Titum Annium plurimum rei publicae profuisse, maxima laetitia populum Romanum, cunctam Italiam, nationes omnes adfecisse et dicat et sentiat? non queo vetera illa populi Romani gaudia quanta fuerint iudicare: multas tamen iam summorum imperatorum clarissimas victorias aetas nostra vidit, quarum nulla neque tam diuturnam laetitiam attulit nec tantam.

78. mandate hoc memoriae, iudices. spero multa vos liberosque vestros in re publica bona esse visuros: in eis singulis ita semper existimabitis, vivo Publio Clodio nihil eorum vos visuros fuisse. in spem maximam et (quem ad modum confido) verissimam sumus adducti, hunc ipsum annum, hoc ipso summo viro consule, compressa hominum licentia, cupiditatibus confractis, legibus et iudiciis constitutis, salutarem civitati fore. num quis est igitur tam demens, qui hoc Publio Clodio vivo contingere potuisse arbitretur? quid? ea quae tenetis privata atque vestra, dominante homine furioso quod ius perpetuae possessionis habere potuissent? non timeo, iudices, ne odio inimicitiarum mearum inflammatus libentius haec in illum evomere videar quam verius. etenim si praecipuum esse debebat, tamen ita communis erat omnium ille hostis ut in communi odio paene aequaliter versaretur odium meum. non potest dici satis, ne cogitari quidem, quantum in illo sceleris, quantum exiti fuerit.

79. quin sic attendite, iudices. fingite animis – liberae sunt enim nostrae cogitationes, et quae volunt sic intuentur ut ea cernamus quae non videmus. fingite igitur cogitatione imaginem huius condicionis meae, si possim efficere Milonem ut absolvatis, sed ita: si Publius Clodius revixerit – quid vultu extimuistis? quonam modo ille vos vivus adficeret, quos mortuus inani cogitatione percussit? quid? si ipse Gnaeus Pompeius, qui ea virtute ac fortuna est ut ea potuerit semper quae nemo praeter illum, si is, inquam, potuisset aut quaestionem de morte Publi Clodi ferre aut ipsum ab inferis excitare, utrum putatis potius facturum fuisse? etiam si propter amicitiam vellet illum ab inferis evocare, propter rem publicam non fecisset. eius igitur mortis sedetis ultores, cuius vitam si putetis per vos restitui posse, nolitis; et de eius nece lata quaestio est, qui si lege eadem reviviscere posset, lata lex numquam esset. huius ergo interfector si esset, in confitendo ab eisne poenam timeret quos liberavisset?

80. Graeci homines deorum honores tribuunt eis viris qui tyrannos necaverunt. quae ego vidi Athenis, quae aliis in urbibus Graeciae! quas res divinas talibus institutas viris! quos cantus, quae carmina! prope ad immortalitatis et religionem et memoriam consecrantur. vos tanti conservatorem populi, tanti sceleris ultorem non modo honoribus nullis adficietis, sed etiam ad supplicium rapi patiemini? confiteretur, confiteretur, inquam, si fecisset, et magno animo et libenter, se fecisse libertatis omnium causa quod esset non confitendum modo, sed etiam vere praedicandum.

Commentary Notes

Sections 1–23

Cicero begins the speech nervously, noting the presence of armed soldiers surrounding the court. He reassures his audience that they are there to prevent any violent behaviour, not to encourage it, and to ensure that the trial proceeds and concludes in an orderly manner.

He also talks about the circumstances that led the Senate, instead of relying on existing laws and legal procedures, to set up a special court for this particular case. He pays tribute to Pompey, the consul, for his good sense in arranging this, and compliments the members of the jury and the president of the court for the integrity of character which led them to be chosen.

He is not going to dispute the fact that Milo did indeed kill Clodius, but he points out that killing a man does not in itself imply guilt and make a conviction for murder inevitable; there are situations when it is not against the law to kill someone, most obviously when it is done in self-defence. So, he says, the only question before the court is who attacked whom; and he proceeds to explain what led up to the fateful encounter between the two men.

Section 24

qui non . . .: keep sight of the structure of this elaborate sentence:

(i) **cum statuisset . . . gerere posset**: a *cum*-clause, giving Clodius' basic reason for taking the action he did;

(ii) a pause – and then this section from **qui** to **quaereret**, giving
      further reasons for Clodius' behaviour – and heightening
      expectation, as he has not yet said *what* it was he did;
(iii) the 'main clause', beginning dramatically with **subito**;
(iv) from **non, ut fit . . .** a section further explaining Clodius'
      purpose in becoming a candidate for a different year.

scelere: Cicero uses this word vaguely ('type of wickedness'), to
suggest that in his praetorship Clodius would have shown complete
disregard for the constitution and used violent means to get his
programme of legislation through.

anno superiore probably means 54 BC, when the elections for 53
should have been held. As they were not held until 53 itself, Clodius
would not have had long enough in office to do all he wanted.

ita . . . ut . . .: it is hardly necessary to translate the *ita* introducing the
Result Clause ('. . . with the result that . . .').

The *subjunctives* **spectaret, vellet** and **quaereret** are there because after
qui they are giving *reasons* for Clodius' decision; this is a regular usage.

non honoris gradum spectaret: Clodius wanted more out of his
praetorship than just the distinction of holding the office.

sed et . . . et . . .: there were two objections in his mind (**et . . . et . . .**)
about continuing to be a candidate for 53 BC.

conlegam: 'as his colleague'.

singulari virtute: an 'ablative of description'.

ad dilacerandam rem publicam (and below, **ad praeturam gerendam**
and **ad evertendam rem publicam**): *ad* with a gerund or gerundive
expression is a common and compact way of expressing *purpose* ('in
order to tear the state apart').

annum suum: 'his' year, in the sense of the one that was 'right for him', i.e. the earliest year in which he could have stood.

in proximum: <*annum*> should be understood.

ut fit: 'as (normally) happens', 'as is the usual explanation' when candidates withdraw.

religione aliqua: *religio* does not normally mean 'religion', but a technicality associated with religious ritual – here a 'religious objection'. The ablative gives a reason, as often. The sort of objection Cicero has in mind would be a declaration by the priests as the election was about to begin that the omens were unfavourable or some other technical objection linked to the very formal Roman state religion.

ut haberet . . ., the real explanation. **quod ipse dicebat**: *quod* = 'what/ the thing which' = 'as . . .'. **hoc est**: 'that is to say', 'in other words'.

Section 25

occurrebat: the imperfect tense is significant; this was not a sudden thought, but something which started to enter Clodius' calculations when his basic plan – to switch to another year – was seeming so attractive.

futuram = *futuram esse*.

consule Milone is equivalent to a conditional clause, 'if Milo were consul' (literally 'with Milo as consul').

fieri, the *present* infinitive, reflects the way Milo was 'in process of becoming' consul.

contulit se: *se conferre* is to 'take oneself off to', 'go off to'. It implies a deliberate action with some plan in mind.

AS

The use of **eius** and not part of *suus* makes it perfectly clear that *Milo's* rivals are meant. Milo was one of three candidates for the office; Clodius hoped to arrange for the election of the other two and so exclude Milo.

invitis illis: like *consule Milone*, 'if . . .'

ita . . . ut . . .: 'in such a way that . . .', introducing a Result Clause, means that Clodius was setting his own conditions for helping these two candidates.

Note that **suis** is emphatic because possessive adjectives (*suus, noster* etc.) generally follow their nouns; if they precede, they are emphatic.

dictitabat: *dictito* is a 'frequentative' form of *dico*, implying that 'he repeatedly said'. The cliché about 'carrying it on his own shoulders' was therefore presumably one that Clodius himself had become known for using as a kind of catchphrase – Cicero may be ridiculing him for his unoriginal form of words.

tribus: accusative plural of the word for 'tribe'. The people were organized into 35 voting units (called 'tribes', but this is not in any sense a racial division), and at this period there was a highly organized system for bribing a tribe to deliver its block vote. Presumably Clodius summoned those who acted as the tribes' representatives for this purpose, not the entire tribes.

se interponebat: 'he made himself the go-between'.

Collinam novam: feminine because the word for 'tribe', which is feminine, is to be understood. There was already a *Collina* tribe, so quite what Clodius was scheming is unclear; indeed, the imperfect **conscribebat** suggests only that a plan was evolving – Clodius was all for forming a new tribe, but it never actually became a reality.

quanto ... tanto ...: a 'correlative' clause, like our expression 'the more, the merrier'. *quanto* and *tanto* are neuter ablatives, 'by how much <the more> ... , by so much <the more> ...'

ille is Clodius, **hic** is Milo; Cicero preserves this distinction between them by means of *hic* and *ille* at many points in the speech and it will be very helpful to remember this.

vidit ... fortissimum virum ... certissimum consulem: understand *esse* (or *futurum esse*), coming before *certissimum*, to complete the Indirect Statement. **certissimum** is virtually an adverb ('an absolute certainty as consul' = 'was most definitely ...').

sermonibus goes not with **intellexit** (for which *e sermonibus* would probably be needed) but with **esse declaratum**, as the arrangement of words (**non solum ... sed etiam**) makes clear.

suffragiis: in the elections that it had been impossible to complete.

Section 26

Etruriamque: Clodius had maintained what was virtually a military base in this area to the north of Rome.

vexarat = *vexaverat*. Any regular first conjugation verb can shorten its perfect-stem tenses by dropping the *-vi-* or *-ve-* syllable (so *portasti, portarunt, portaram, portassem* etc.).

ex Appennino: the Apennines are a mountain range that forms the 'spine' of Italy. (There can be one *p* or two in the Latin word's spelling.)

quos videbatis: *quos* is more a 'connecting relative' than a true descriptive one, and adds a further point – not so much 'whom you saw' as '– and you saw them' (regularly, implied by the imperfect tense).

A S

res erat . . .: the **res** refers not to the presence of these gangs in Rome, but to Clodius' plot to kill Milo. In reading, a pause before *res* will make this clear – and the *etenim* clause confirms it.

etenim is a connecting word almost always used (as here) to give an illustration or a more detailed explanation of a statement just made.

consulatum Miloni eripi non posse, vitam posse: the balance between **consulatum** and **vitam** produces a contrast between the two clauses; the comma after *non posse* can be felt as a 'but'.

quaerenti ex eo: 'asking him'; *quaero* means to seek information rather than 'ask someone', which is therefore *quaero e/ex*.

spe: *spes* here is in the sense of 'expectation', 'prospects'.

triduo, quadriduo: ablatives of 'time within which'. **summum** is adverbial, 'at most'.

Section 27

erat: perhaps 'would have been', rather than 'was' (when imagined conditions have a neuter idea as the subject rather than an actual noun – here, 'it would not have been difficult' – it is not necessary for the subjunctive to be used).

necessarium: the word might seem to be redundant after **legitimum**, but (i) Cicero is at all times concerned to make it clear that Milo's journey was obligatory for him, whereas Clodius' was entirely a matter of his choice, and (ii) with the two preceding words, it produces an emphatic 'tricolon'.

Lanuvium: the place, in fact, where Milo had grown up, a community about 32 kilometres (20 miles) from Rome.

AS

dictator: merely a technical term for the senior magistrate (like a mayor) at Lanuvium and many other Italian towns. It will have been an ancient title.

Lanuvi is probably locative ('at Lanuvium'), though it could be genitive (singular place-names of the First or Second Declension use the genitive ending for their locative).

quod re intellectum est: quod = 'a thing which', 'as'; **re** is well translated by Plaistowe and Masom (followed by Colson) as 'the sequel'.

ita profectus est ut . . .: 'in such a way that . . .' sounds artificial; 'the circumstances of his departure were (such) that . . .'

eius furor: in an ordinary relative clause, *eius* rather than *suus* is normal, even where, as happens here, it refers reflexively to the subject of the main clause.

habita est: *habeo* is a natural word to use of 'delivering' a speech (*orationem habeo*) or, as here, 'holding' a meeting (*contionem habeo*).

obire: 'to be there at the . . .'.

Section 28

autem: Cicero is from now on continually concerned to point out the differences in the behaviour and characters of the two men.

dimissus: a normal word for terminating a meeting ('dismissed' could be misleading).

ut fit: 'as happens', 'as is normal'; a humorous touch (it had a more sarcastic edge in §24).

profectus = *profectus est*.

AS

id temporis: not quite 'at that time' (for which *eo tempore* would be the natural Latin) but 'at that point in the day (when …)'; the relationship between the timings of the two men's movements is something Cicero is most concerned to establish.

redire potuisset: though the meaning is 'could have …', Latin always uses a *present* infinitive with *possum* (and with *debeo*).

si quidem: 'if in fact …'; *quidem* is sarcastic and sows an early seed of doubt about Clodius' intentions that afternoon.

ut solebat highlights how unusual the absence of an entourage of decadent Greeks was for Clodius; **quod numquam fere** <*faciebat*> is similarly a footnote on *sine uxore*. The list works up to a climax.

hic is Milo (as almost always). In Cicero's eyes, an **insidiator** is exactly what he is not; Cicero's technique would be clear from the sarcastic tone of voice he will have used for *insidiator*, and confirmed grammatically by the subjunctive **apparasset** (= *apparavisset*), which he uses to distance himself from the allegation.

impedito: Clodius was *expeditus*, but Milo's retinue was 'encumbered', 'restricted in its movement'. These boys and girls presumably were a choir Milo was taking with him for the ceremony the next day.

Section 29

non multo secus: 'or not far off'. **multo** is an ablative of the neuter *multum*, 'not differently *by much*'; it is common in expressions like *non multo post*, 'not long afterwards', and is called the 'ablative of measure of difference'.

in hunc: Milo.

adversi (from *adverto*): *se adverterunt* would mean 'they turned' (as *(ad)verto* is a transitive verb, *se* is necessary to give correct sense); so for a perfect participle, *adversi* (the perfect participle passive) is used for 'having turned towards . . .'

reiecta paenula: ablative absolute, very suitable for Milo's brisk reaction.

acri animo: 'with a keen spirit' is virtually an adverb, 'vigorously'.

illi qui erant cum Clodio: not the same as the group who had charged down from the hillside and **raedarium occidunt**.

recurrere and **caedere** are with **incipiunt**.

putarent: the use of a subjunctive here is slightly illogical. If Cicero had written *quod hic iam interfectus esset*, the subjunctive *interfectus esset* would have conveyed the feeling that this was the *slaves'* belief; or he could have written *quod hunc iam interfectum putabant* to make this clearer; but in fact he has combined the two. The same oddity is often found with *dico* (*quod dicerent* etc.), and no great significance is to be found in it. It is rather like when we say, 'he went away, because he said it was late,' meaning 'he went away because it was late (and he said so)'.

ex quibus qui . . .: **quibus** is the group of slaves just referred to; **qui** = *ei qui*.

animo fideli . . . fuerunt: a description of these slaves, using the 'ablative of description'.

pugnari: the infinitive of the impersonal *pugnatur*, 'fighting was going on.'

prohiberentur . . .: this is within a lengthy **cum** clause, with four subjunctive verbs, of which this is only the second.

AS

The vague **id** is eventually explained by **quod** ('what . . .').

derivandi criminis causa: *causa* following a genitive expression means 'for the sake/purpose of . . .' and is very often found with a gerund(ive).

criminis: *crimen* means usually a 'criminal charge', and much less often a 'crime'; here it is the 'guilt' or 'responsibility' for incurring a possible *crimen*.

ut factum est: **ut** = 'as' ('I shall describe it *ut factum est*').

nec imperante . . .: an ablative absolute expression, with three participles, all in the present tense.

suos quisque servos . . .: **suos** goes with **servos** ('each person/ anyone . . . his own slaves') with **quisque** 'interrupting' the phrase; this is standard word-order when part of *suus* is used to reinforce *quisque*.

voluisset: 'would have . . .', the 'potential' use of the subjunctive (an 'if . . .' clause like 'if they had been asked' can be understood).

Section 30

sicuti = *sicut*: the **ita** simply answers the **sicuti** (perhaps reinforcing it: 'exactly as . . . .') and does not need to be translated.

gesta sunt: 'happened', a common meaning of the vague *gero*.

vi = Milo's 'violence': **vis** = Clodius' attempted violence.

oppressa is nominative: *audacia oppressa est virtute*.

nihil dico . . .: understand *dico* with each **nihil**, and *consequor* with **vos** and with **omnes boni**.

id: '(saying) this' (how lucky we are to be rid of Clodius).

The subjunctive usage in **prosit** (from *prosum*, which takes the dative) is the potential use – '<if I did>, it would not ...'. It is nothing to do with the preceding Indirect Questions.

qui hoc fato ... servaret: this is a difficult sentence.

(i)   **ut** introduces a result clause; the perfect subjunctive (**potuerit** here) is quite usual in a result clause to denote a single, momentary, rather than continuing, result – which is wanted here, as Cicero is referring to the particular time when Milo killed Clodius (or rather his slaves did, according to the version he is giving).

(ii) **quin una ... servaret**, word-for-word = '(could not) ... but that he also ... saved'; the 'but that' is old-fashioned, and a natural way of translating this and most other *quin*-clauses is 'without ...': 'without also saving ...'
The statement, explaining the destiny that Milo was born with – its effect was that he could not help doing things which simultaneously (**una**) benefited the state – is really relatively detached from what precedes, as though the sentence ran *nihil sane id prosit Miloni; is enim hoc fato ...* – it is a footnote to what Cicero is saying about the irrelevance of talking about the benefits that come from Clodius' death.

iure 'justifiably', 'with justification' (*iure*, the ablative of *ius*, is used as an adverb).

defendam, subjunctive, for a type of Result Clause – 'I have nothing such that I can offer it as a defence.'

sin hoc ... praescripsit: **ratio/necessitas/mos/natura** are all subjects of **praescripsit**, and the datives with them are all groups who have had the rule given to them; it would probably be better in translation to turn things round and make these groups the subjects, 'if intelligent beings have been commanded by reason ...'. **hoc** is the object of **praescripsit**, and points forward (as did **hoc fato** above) to the **ut ...** clause (which this time is an Indirect Command).

caput often means 'life' (in English we talk about 'capital punishment') and so **vita** is only a synonym.

quin simul . . .: 'without at the same time ...' (see above on *quin*).

inciderint is most likely a perfect subjunctive, and, if so, it is subjunctive because it is in a clause which is part of Indirect Speech (the verb in such clauses generally drops into a subjunctive), and perfect tense because it stands for the future perfect that would have been used if it had not been in Indirect Speech – literally, 'those who shall have fallen among robbers'; the use is like that in a conditional clause, and indeed this is virtually equivalent to 'if they fall among...'.

Section 31

quod si . . . = 'But if ...'

ita = that you, the jury, would not accept a plea of self-defence.

Milo is the subject of **putasset** (= *putavisset*: all regular first conjugation verbs can shorten their *-aviss-* parts to *-ass-*).

Now although **putasset** is subjunctive, and the conditional is quite obviously of the 'would/should' ('unreal') type, the main verb **fuit** is not subjunctive but indicative; when in the main clause of an unreal conditional the subject is the impersonal 'it' (and therefore likely to be with a neuter singular adjective, as it is here), the verb goes into the indicative instead of the subjunctive. This does not affect the English translation – which is still 'it would have been ...'

non semel ... neque tum primum: the second reference to time ('nor was this the first time') sounds as though it should be something being added to the first, as you would expect from **neque ...**, but there is actually no difference between the two claims; it is just rhetorical repetition with a longer wording to drive the point home.

petitum: *peto* in the sense of 'go for', 'target'.

iugulandum: the gerundive of a verb fills the vacancy in Latin for a present/future passive participle, 'going to be slaughtered'.

quia se non iugulandum illi tradidisset: Milo would have been executed by the jury precisely for *not* having let himself be executed by Clodius instead. **tradidisset** indicates that this would have been an idea in *other people's* minds.

vestrum: genitive of *vos*. There are two genitives of *vos*: *vestrum* is always used with numbers or the equivalent ('three of you', 'some of you', 'none of you'), and *vestri* in all other situations (e.g. with verbs or adjectives that take the genitive). (The genitives *nostrum* and *nostri* work in the same way.)

hoc = *ita*, slightly repetitive.

illud: points forward to the Indirect Questions (**occisusne sit ...**) that follow; it is not necessary to translate a pronoun that has this 'anticipatory' function.

in iudicium: 'before the court'.

occisusne sit = *num occisus sit*; Indirect Questions are often indicated by the *-ne* suffix, as though they were actual questions rather than indirect, but the verb will still be a subjunctive.

quod fatemur ... quod multis ...: *quod* both times means 'something which'.

AS

causis: 'cases', 'trials'.

id est quod: 'it is this which . . . '

contra rem publicam factum iudicavit: it is an embarrassment to Cicero that just two or three weeks before the trial, the Senate had passed a decree stating that the killing of Clodius had been *contra rem publicam*, against the interests of the Republic. Pompey as consul had then passed a law (**latum est** from the term *legem fero* for 'to have a law passed') that a special enquiry should be held into this (**quaereretur, quaestionem tulit**). Cicero here argues that Pompey was not pre-judging the case but wanting to establish the circumstances and legality of what had happened.

factae sint: the subject is **insidiae**.

de hoc: 'on this question'.

rem contrasts with **hominem**, and **iure** with **facto**; here **iure** (normally 'justifiably') means '(the question of) justification'.

quaestionem tulit: the *quaestio* was established by a special law, so *fero* is an appropriate verb.

num quid = 'surely-not (*num*) anything' = 'surely nothing'. Latin often brings negatives to the very front of a sentence, and *quis*, rather than *aliquis* or any other word, is used for 'anyone' after *ne*, after *num* in any of its meanings, and after *si* or *nisi*.

profecto: 'assuredly', 'without doubt'. Cicero answers his own question.

hic = Milo; **ille** = Clodius – as virtually always throughout the speech.

ut ne sit . . .: these are generally taken by editors as two result clauses ('this question comes before the court; with the result, if answered one way, that Milo will not go unpunished . . .'). Although generally not *ne* but *non* is used to negative a result clause, there seem to be other examples of exceptions. However, they may be commands ('let Milo not go unpunished . . .).

scelere: *scelus* here is not the 'wicked deed', but 'wickedness', 'guilt'.

Section 32

quonam igitur pacto . . .: *quo pacto* is regular Latin for 'in what way'; the *-nam* suffix indicates incredulity or exasperation ('what on earth . . . !'); there is a slight note of sarcasm here, as Cicero believes it will be extremely easy for this to be proved.

in illa quidem . . .: *quidem* often conveys the idea of 'on the one hand'; Cicero will deal with Clodius first, and Milo, and his lack of motive, later.

illa, though actually agreeing with **belua**, still refers to Clodius, as *ille*, by itself, almost invariably does.

docere: to 'explain <that . . .>'.

propositam: 'set before' him, 'apparent'.

illud Cassianum: 'that favourite question of Cassius', a lawyer from over sixty years before, famous for his dictum *cui bono?*, 'to whom was it (for) the good?' (using the predicative dative expression *bono est* 'it is an advantage'), 'who stood to gain?' **fuerit** is a perfect subjunctive because the three words form an Indirect Question.

persona is not quite 'person', but 'the type of character someone is'; the word has its origins in the theatre and originally meant the mask through which (*per-*) an actor sounded (*sonare*) his lines; 'dramatis personae' is sometimes used to mean the 'characters' in a play, the 'cast-list'.

AS

etsi boni . . .: he means that good men (like Milo) do not succumb to any temptation to do wrong, however much they stand to gain from it. Notice the contrast between **boni** and **improbi**, and the more interesting one between **nullo** and **saepe parvo**.

atqui (not the same as *atque*; more like *at*) **. . . –** it was not a *minor* temptation that Clodius felt (**emolumento . . . parvo**), but something vitally affecting his immediate future and his plans for radical, perhaps revolutionary, actions.

adsequebatur: the use of the imperfect tense conveys the idea that this was what Clodius was in a position to gain, if Milo were killed.

non eo consule: just as Clodius was a candidate for the praetorship, so Milo was standing for the consulship. **non eo consule** is like an ablative absolute (as is **eis consulibus** below), literally 'not with (= without) that man being consul', the **eo** being picked up immediately by **quo** ('with whom <as consul>').

Take **sceleris** with **nihil**, 'nothing in the way of crime', 'no crime at all' (more general than *nullum scelus*).

si non . . . at . . . certe: 'if not actually (= perhaps not actually) . . . yet at any rate' (*certe* with the preceding word **coniventibus**, not with **speraret**).

eludere: the prefix strengthens the basic meaning of the verb, 'to have the greatest possible enjoyment'.

furoribus: *furor*, 'frenzy', would normally only be found in the singular; the use of the plural here suggests 'wild acts' which are schemed (**cogitatis**) by Clodius. **illis** means 'those we all know' (a similar use to that in **illud Cassianum** above).

cuius (= Clodius') belongs with **conatus**, which is from the fourth declension noun *conatus –ūs* (m), here in the accusative plural. **illi** are the consuls Clodius would like to have seen in office.

AS

debere is here in its basic sense of 'to owe'; the imagined **beneficium** is Clodius' getting them elected to their consulships. Take **conroboratam** with **vetustate**, 'strengthened by . . .'. **audacia** is rarely, in Cicero, an admirable quality, and this affects the translation.

Section 33

Cicero rounds on a henchman of Clodius, accusing him of possessing documents which would reveal the terrifying programme of legislation Clodius intended to pass in his praetorship.

Section 34

interfuerit: *interest*, 'it concerns, makes a difference', takes a genitive of the person whose interests are affected (or a possessive pronoun in the feminine ablative: *meā interest*, 'it concerns me'); the ablative *re* is understood in both usages (hence the genitive). Another impersonal verb *refert* has the same meaning and the same construction.

quid erat cur . . .: 'what reason was there for . . .'

✷ 'The killing of Clodius' is the object of **admitteret** and **optaret**; with **non dicam**, Cicero is choosing his words carefully.

'obstabat . . .': an answer that might be given by an opponent of Milo.

at begins a very strong denial of this.

eo repugnante: **eo** is Clodius. **fiebat** <*consul*>. The second **eo** goes with **magis**, 'more by this fact', 'all the more'. **immo vero** is a strong 'indeed', implying the contradiction of what has preceded.

✷ **nec me suffragatore meliore . . .:** in popular perception, Cicero was one of Milo's principal supporters (*suffragator*); here he ingeniously sidesteps the unpopularity this brought him in some quarters by suggesting that Clodius was a still greater electoral asset; **me** is emphatic. **utebatur**: *utor* has idiomatic meanings not covered by the English 'use'. Here, 'he did not have *me* as . . .'

apud vos: 'with you'. *apud*, a vague preposition, has a range of meanings centring on 'among/with'.

sine . . .: the question began as *quis . . . erat . . . qui sibi . . . proponeret*, 'who could visualize . . . ?'; as the answer is 'no-one', the (rhetorical) question is regarded as negative; so no-one would regard Clodius' praetorship, if no controls were placed on it, as without . . ., i.e. it would be certain to lead to revolution (*res novae*).

proponeret: *quis erat qui . . .* is felt to introduce a result clause ('the type of person who would . . .'). **auderet** and **posset** in the next sentence are also (probably) to be regarded as in a Result Clause introduced by *esset is consul qui . . .*

★ **solutam**: referring to Clodius' imagined praetorship, 'unrestrained'.

fore: alternative future infinitive of *sum* (brisker than *futuram esse*), 'would be'.

quis dubitaret . . .: 'potential subjunctive, 'who would . . .'

at nunc: 'but now', 'but as it is'; *nunc* often marks a change in the situation, as here.

rebus: here 'methods'.

enitendum est Miloni: the 'obligation' gerund, with the dative of the person who must act.

ut tueatur dignitatem suam: a slightly odd expression, 'to protect his standing'; Cicero means that Milo still intended to aim at the consulship, a position to which he felt entitled. Notice this meaning of *dignitas*, not 'dignity', but whatever 'rank' someone has in society.

uni: the dative singular (with *huic*) of *unus* (genitive *unius*, dative *uni*).

cecidit: 'has fallen', 'is his no more'.

adepti estis (*adipiscor*) is followed by a clause, *ne quem civem metueretis*, the advantage they have won (**ne quem** = 'that you ... no-one'); it contrasts with **hic ... perdidit**, taking accusative objects. **exercitationem**: '<scope to> exercise/display (his worth)'. **suffragationem**: rather abstract ('electoral support'), so as to be parallel to **exercitationem**.

temptari: not the normal meaning of 'try' here, but a near-synonym for **labefactari** with which it is contrasted in this sentence.

coeptus est: when the infinitive with *coepi* is passive, *coepi* itself also goes into the passive; we would not try to reproduce this slightly odd behaviour of *coepi* in translation, but it is the normal Latin usage.

prodest ... obest ...: a neat contrast, using the rarer *obsum* rather than *obsto*.

Section 35

'**at valuit ...** ': the (imaginary) objection here is that Milo, in killing Clodius, might not have been acting rationally, but under the force of powerful emotions – hatred, anger etc. **at** (or *at enim*) regularly introduces such imaginary counter-arguments.

valuit: literally 'was strong'; Milo's hatred 'was dominant'. Notice the use of the perfect tense for 'on this one occasion'.

fecit: 'he acted ...'; 'the deed' is understood as the object.

iniuriae: all the wrong Clodius had ever done to Milo; Milo now had the chance to pay him back. **punitor doloris sui** conveys the same idea.

The isolated **quid?** means 'what about this next point?', 'here is my point'.

si haec non dico: this is quite a difficult sentence. **haec** are these 'feelings' of *odium*, being *iratus* etc. **haec maiora fuerunt in Clodio** (= 'in the case of Clodius') **quam in Milone** is what Cicero might have been expected to argue. In fact he will go one better and not say this (**non dico**), but assert boldly that while such emotions were actually not **maiora** but **maxima** in the case of Clodius, they were (more importantly) non-existent (**nulla**) in Milo. If he can succeed in proving this deliberately difficult version of his position, surely the jury must be convinced (**quid vultis amplius?**).

quid enim odisset . . .: 'why would Milo have hated . . .'.

segetem ac materiam suae gloriae: this re-states the argument already advanced in the preceding section, that Milo needed Clodius to be sure of being elected consul. Notice the emphasis, by position, of **suae**.

praeter hoc civile odium quo . . .: quo: '<hatred> with which we hate . . .'; this seems a rather lame way of saying 'obviously all right-minded people hated Clodius; Milo did hate him, but not to any greatly exaggerated degree – not so much that he lost control of himself and killed him in a rage.'

omnes makes sense as either nominative ('we all . . .') or accusative ('we hate all . . .'); the first is stronger and more likely, as it then explains **civile odium**.

illi erat ut . . .: illi is dative, 'he (= Clodius) had good reason to . . .'

defensorem . . . are all roles in which Clodius would have cast Milo, and have hated him for it. **primum** 'firstly' (adverb, not adjective with *defensorem*, which would not make sense, and in any case **deinde** follows).

defensorem salutis meae: a reference to Milo's part in Cicero's recall from exile, of which much more is to be said soon. **furoris** and **armorum suorum** describe the way Clodius controlled Rome with his armed gangs.

reus Milonis: literally 'a defendant of Milo', means 'made into a defendant by Milo', i.e. 'accused by Milo'.

hoc seems to refer just to the last item on Cicero's list (his impending trial on the charge made against him by Milo), or it might mean 'this behaviour of Milo' in a quite general way. **tyrannum** because Clodius is a law to himself, and loathes the idea of being restrained by Milo.

iniusto . . . iustum: a play on words with nothing very deep behind it. Clodius is *iniustus*; granted which, it is not very surprising if he hated Milo; so his hatred is 'actually justified' under the morality in reverse by which he lives.

Sections 36–42

Cicero argues that Clodius was by nature a man of violence, and lists a number of episodes when well-known figures had been threatened with death, or actually killed, by him or his supporters. Milo's character was quite the opposite, he says, and he gives numerous examples of occasions when he could have killed Clodius quite justifiably – and would have earned enormous gratitude by doing so. But he would not have killed him on the Appian Way, in circumstances where this would have been impossible to justify, especially when he needed to keep his reputation intact with the prospect of elections very soon.

Section 43

igitur adds a note of sarcasm.

diem campi means 'the day he would go to the Campus Martius' (where the elections were held).

From **cruentis** this must be a rhetorical question – Cicero cannot be saying that Milo did have bloodstained hands but asking whether he was really likely to remain a candidate if he had blood on his hands.

scelus = **facinus**, a repetition for emphasis; if Milo had been guilty, Cicero suggests, it would indeed have been a terrible crime.

prae se ferens: literally 'carrying in front of him ...' = 'advertising ...' (**prae**, which takes the ablative, is one of the rarer prepositions; it usually means, as it does here, 'in front of').

The **auspicia**, 'auspices', are taken by religious officials as an election or any other public business begins, to check on whether the gods approve of what is about to be done. The 'centuries' (**centuriarum**) are the groups into which the people are arranged for voting purposes.

The tense of **veniebat** is significant, 'was he coming ...?' i.e. 'was he likely to come ...?'

quam ... non credibile: an exclamation – 'how impossible to believe!' The first **hoc** is the idea that Milo would have dared to kill Clodius with the elections so near. It is the neuter nominative singular (*hŏc*), whereas the second **hoc** is the ablative singular (masculine) (*hōc*).

in hoc, ... in Clodio ...: in = 'in the case of ...'

non dubitandum: 'not to be doubted', the opposite of **non credibile** earlier.

idem (not the masculine *īdem* but the neuter *ĭdem*) means rather more than 'the same thing'. Here and commonly in oratory, any part of *idem, eadem, idem* can be found doing the work of 'at the same time' (or 'and also'), reinforcing a point by adding something, often (as here) something which contrasts with the original point.

quid?: see note on §35, a common device in oratory.

caput: probably with **audaciae**, and meaning 'the source of'. *audacia* (literally 'boldness') means 'outrageous behaviour', not stopping to consider the consequences.

Take **peccandi** with **inlecebram**, and **impunitatis** with **spem**.

haec is the *spes* just referred to.

in utro igitur . . .: perhaps another sarcastic *igitur*.

ut eum nihil delectaret . . .: *eum*, not *se*, because in Result Clauses the reflexive pronoun is not used to refer back to the original subject of the sentence; in this respect Result Clauses differ from Purpose Clauses. Nor do Result Clauses begin with *ne* when they are negative (we have here *ut . . . nihil*).

per naturam: 'naturally', 'of itself'.

quod aut per naturam fas esset aut per leges liceret: natural law and actual systems of law between them cover the whole field of what limits a person's actions and stops him behaving entirely without restraints. Clodius, says Cicero, took a perverse pleasure in ignoring every single one of the constraints that normally apply. **fas esset** and **liceret** are broadly equivalent, but **fas** carries overtones of what the gods allow and belongs more to the realm of general morality.

AS

Section 44

quid = 'why . . .?'.

Quintus Petilius and Marcus Porcius Cato are evidently members of the jury, which at this stage in the trial would have numbered eighty-one, chosen by a random selection process (*sors* = 'chance') from an even larger panel. Nothing else is known of Petilius, but Cato was a significant figure, a staunch conservative who became a martyr to his cause when he committed suicide in 46 BC (in the Civil War) rather than live in a Rome dominated by Julius Caesar.

divina quaedam sors: 'a kind of divine chance'. It is very common to find *quidam* used between an adjective and a noun like this; the pronoun fills the phrase out and emphasizes the describing word – 'a quite providentially lucky method of selection'.

Marcus Favonius is another obscure figure, but the detail Cicero is reporting here is something he has already mentioned, in §26.

vivo Clodio: an ablative absolute, 'while . . .' (Latin does not have a participle for 'being').

triduo: ablative of 'time within which'. It really means in *two* rather than three days, because of the Romans' practice of 'inclusive' counting; if today is Thursday, then on this system, Saturday is three days ahead (Thursday, Friday, Saturday – three days), whereas we reckon in 24-hour periods and would call it only two days.

post diem tertium gesta res est quam dixerat: gesta est is just 'happened'; **post . . . quam** is just *postquam* (such separation of *post/quam, prius/quam* and *ante/quam* is quite common). *die tertio* would have been expected (ablative of 'time when'), but has dropped into the accusative, slightly illogically, because *post* takes the accusative and it would have been strange to see it apparently with a different case.

cum ille . . .: **ille**, as usual, is Clodius.

Section 45

dies non fefellit: the 'day' is the day Clodius was apparently saying Milo would die, the 'date'. This date 'did not deceive' Clodius – he got it right, and his plan was to attack him on that day.

equidem: another strengthening 'particle', ('indeed'), but only used with the first person; it may be a contraction of *ego quidem*.

dixi equidem modo: this was in §27, where he described his departure from Rome.

nosse = *novisse* (from *nosco noscere novi notum*, found more usually as the compound *cognosco . . . cognitum*). *nosco* strictly means 'I get to know', so *novi* = 'I have got to know', 'I know', a present tense meaning.

negoti nihil: 'nothing of a problem', 'not at all difficult'.

ut ante dixi: in §27.

A **contio** was an official meeting of the people which could be summoned by a tribune (or other magistrate), who would preside at it. The purpose of these gatherings, which seem to have become very frequent in the late 50s BC, was almost always for the tribune and perhaps others of the same opinion to harangue the people on a topical issue. They did not result in votes or decisions, though it was common for them to be held before elections or a vote on some item of legislation. The speeches must often have been of a highly personal character, and supporters of the politician being attacked might very well turn up, increasing the chances of the occasion going out of control and turning to violence.

ipsius: of Clodius. The word seems to link with **mercennario**, and if this means 'bribed' (adjective), the words together mean 'bribed by Clodius himself' (and the genitive **ipsius** could be called a 'subjective genitive', as *ipse* does the bribing). (Some editors – partly because of the genitive – think that **mercennario** must be a noun, and would translate 'by that agent of himself, a tribune of the people', but this reads rather weakly, especially as usually tribunes called a *contio* in any case.)

quem . . . quam . . . quos . . .: these are just 'connecting' relatives ('this meeting . . .').

illi: with **fuit**, at the end of the sentence ('he had . . .'). Some editors omit *fuit* from the text (the dative *illi* so obviously implies it), and it may be felt to read better without it.

etiam: 'even', 'actually'.

exeundi: from *exeo*, the gerund ('going away'), in the genitive (with **causa**, 'a reason for . . .').

Notice the genitives (**itineris, manendi, exeundi**) with words meaning 'reason (for . . .)', 'opportunity (for . . .)', 'need (for . . .)'; this is a standard use of the genitive when a noun (**itineris** etc.) depends on another noun (**causa** etc.).

quid si . . .: 'and what if this <were true>?', 'can't we suppose that . . .?' Cicero tries to clinch this last part of the argument by contrasting the men's differing knowledge of one another's movements on the fateful day.

ut . . . sic . . .: 'just as Clodius . . . , so Milo . . .'; there is a contrast between the two clauses, so we could translate 'although Clodius . . . , Milo on the other hand . . .'. 'Although' can be yet another meaning of *ut*.

AS

With **Clodium** understand **fore eo die in via** from the previous clause.

fore = *futurum esse*, the shorter and neater form of the future infinitive of *sum*.

Section 46

qui is occasionally not part of *qui quae quod* but an adverb, 'how?'

quod: 'a question which . . . '

idem (neuter here, ĭdem): the rhetorical use of *idem* again, 'which same question . . .', 'a question which in fact . . .'.

in Clodio: **in**, as often, means 'in the case of'.

ut . . . rogasset: the subject is Clodius, carried over from **in Clodio**; Latin usually marks a change of subject more clearly (e.g. with *ille*), but it is not needed here as Cicero is obviously already dealing with the question he has just raised, of how Clodius would have known about Milo's movements.

rogasset (= *rogavisset*) because this is a loose kind of Result Clause ('for him only to have asked') and though these generally have present, imperfect or sometimes perfect subjunctives, they occasionally need a pluperfect subjunctive to give the right sense.

We know nothing else about *Titus Patina*. Presumably he was an associate of Clodius who also happened to come from Milo's home town of Lanuvium.

familiarissimum: the adjective *familiaris* means 'in someone's immediate circle', his *familia* (which is not just 'family', but includes friends and even slaves), and the word can therefore easily be used as though it were a noun ('relative', 'associate', 'slave'). This makes it possible for the noun here to become a superlative, like an adjective, 'his very close friend'.

Lanuvi: the locative case of Lanuvium, 'at Lanuvium'.

sed ...: a 'throwaway' comment; he could have asked Patina, but in fact there were many others who could have told him the same thing.

permulti: many words can take *per-* as a prefix to intensify the meaning; here 'very many'.

quaesierit ... corruperit: just as present subjunctives can mean 'let him ask!' etc. (the 'Jussive Subjunctive'), so a perfect subjunctive can mean 'let him have asked'. The hypothetical case that Milo did try to find out where Clodius was going is examined.

amicus meus: Arrius is obviously on the other side, so it is not clear whether 'my friend' is sincere, sarcastic or just conventional (like 'my learned friend' in British courts); this last sense does appear elsewhere in Cicero's speeches.

idem (**īdem**, masculine): 'and also'. **comes**: he was actually with Clodius at the time.

in Albano: Clodius owned an estate in the Alban hills, in the countryside outside Rome.

mansurum fuisse: not *mansurum esse*, 'would stay', but *-urum fuisse*, 'would have stayed'. The verb in direct speech would have been the pluperfect subjunctive, *mansisset*, but, for the Indirect Statement, the standard future infinitive would not have represented this clearly enough; so this special form (future participle + *fuisse*) can be used (and this is its only use).

Cyrum architectum: this is the first mention of him and the news brought of his death in the speech, and perhaps is intended as a surprise. Why his death mattered is something Cicero will come to in the next section.

item: 'likewise' goes with **comes**; Causinius and this C. Clodius were both travelling with Clodius.

Section 47

liberatur ... non ... profectus esse: the (not very common) 'nominative + infinitive' construction explains what Milo is acquitted of having done; **non** is redundant and not needed in translating; it is there to emphasize that this is what it has been proved Milo did *not* do. **liberatur** = 'is acquitted' = 'is found not to have').

futurus ... non erat: **futurus** is the future participle of *sum*, '<was not> going to be ...'

deinde = 'secondly', answering the earlier **primum**.

fuisse qui ... dicerent: 'there were those/some who ...'. **dicerent** is subjunctive only because this kind of sentence is regarded as a Result Clause ('people such that they ...', a result).

in hac rogatione suadenda: Milo's trial had required a special bill (*rogatio*) to be passed setting out the rules under which it would be conducted; *suadeo* here is used in a special sense of 'urging' or 'supporting' a proposal.

manu and **consilio** contrast.

maioris alicuius: 'of some more important figure'. As Colson points out, *aliquis* is vaguer and more mysterious than *quidam*.

AS

iacent suis testibus: here *iaceo* means 'to be disproved' (as Colson explains, they are 'floored'!); it is quite common, and although a passive idea, it does not require *a/ab* for the agent.

suis is very emphatic – 'they are disproved by *their own* witnesses', which makes these troublemakers look particularly foolish and best ignored. *suus* and other 'possessive adjectives' (*meus, noster* etc.) normally come after the noun they accompany; when such a possessive word precedes the noun, it is always emphatic.

negant: these are the witnesses, who 'say that Clodius would not have ...'; though 'deny' is the one-word translation of *nego*, 'say ... not ...' is usually a better way of expressing it.

fuisse rediturum = *rediturum fuisse*; 'would have ...' (future participle + *fuisse*, like *mansurum fuisse* in §46).

non vereor ne ...: 'I do not fear that ...', 'I have no further worries that ...'. **quod** with the following **id**, 'a thing which'.

Section 48

occurrit: the present tense, or just possibly the perfect.

illud: 'that (earlier) point'; this is the suggestion (in §46) that Clodius had originally intended to spend the night at his estate in the Alban hills, which appeared to prove that he was not planning an attack on Milo.

ne Clodius quidem: 'not even Clodius' (the usual way of translating *ne ... quidem*) does not make sense; 'Clodius did not ..., either' is better. **quidem** emphasizes **Clodius**.

mansurus: from *maneo*.

AS

si quidem . . .: '<yes,> *if* he . . .' Again, **quidem** emphasizes the word before and gives an incredulous lift to the clause. **si . . . non . . .** is unusual (generally *nisi* is used instead) but makes the **non** very emphatic – 'if he had *not* . . .' (– but he did!)'

exiturus: from *exeo*.

video: in the sense of 'I realise', but a vivid word to use for this, especially in the First Person.

qui dicatur: 'who is said', because the arrival of this apparently unexpected messenger will have been mentioned in the giving of evidence when the trial began or in one of the prosecution speeches that preceded Cicero's.

dicatur is subjunctive only because it is inside a clause that is part of the Indirect Statement.

nuntiasse = *nuntiavisse*.

nuntiaret: 'what would he be reporting . . .?', an imperfect subjunctive, not the pluperfect subjunctive ('what would he have reported . . .?') that we might have expected. Although imperfect subjunctives in conditional sentences usually refer to the present (as in sentences like 'if I knew the answer, I would be a rich man'), sometimes, as here, even in the past the idea of *continuity* is important.

una: 'together with <him>' (**una** is not a case of *unus*, but rather an adverb from it). Cicero, Clodius and the dying architect had been all together in the same room.

simul here is just a variant for *una*.

et illum heredem et me scripserat: it is a reasonable assumption that Cyrus had worked for the two men, perhaps very recently, and so in gratitude he makes them heirs in his will. Surprisingly, heirs could witness wills at this time; later this was not permitted.

AS

quem ... reliquisset: part of the **nuntiabatur** Indirect Statement; the 'original words' would have been 'the man whom you left ...', and in the Indirect Statement this becomes a subjunctive (for a 'subordinate clause inside Indirect Speech', as above with *dicatur*) and drops back in tense to a pluperfect.

eum mortuum ... (= *mortuum esse*): notice the rising tone of incredulity here – **denique** is highly scornful. **postridie hora decima** must go with **nuntiabatur**, not **mortuum**, both because of the word-order and to give the right sense.

Section 49

sit ita factum: 'let it have happened thus', 'suppose it did happen thus'.

in noctem se coniceret: Cicero is about to say more about the dangers of travelling after nightfall.

quid goes with the genitive **festinationis**, literally 'what of hurry', so 'what urgency'.

quod heres erat is the subject of **adferebat**, 'the fact that he was ...'.

properato opus esset clearly means 'there was need to hurry', but using the perfect participle like this to mean the activity ('hurrying') is unusual, especially in Cicero; this is what gerunds are used for. Perhaps this is a slightly colloquial expression.

si quid esset: *quis, quis, quid* after *si* means 'anyone/anything/any'; the subjunctive is because of the conditional, 'if there were any <need>' and instead of continuing 'I would have to ask ...', Cicero directly asks the question. **tandem** not in its usual meaning of 'at last' but as rhetorical vocabulary, 'I ask you', 'please tell me'.

amitteret autem: 'but would lose ...'

vitandus: the gerundive, 'to be avoided' (so with the dative **illi**, 'by him' – datives are usual for the 'agent' ('by …') with gerunds/ gerundives).

cum insidiator esset: 'a would-be atttacker', 'planning to assault him'.

si … sciebat: not 'if he had known' (= *scivisset*), but 'if he did know', a rather bolder way of expressing the argument.

subsidendum atque expectandum: gerunds for what Milo (**Miloni**, dative) should have been doing.

Section 50

neganti: denying that he had intended to intercept Clodius. *nego*, usually 'to say that … not …', here does mean the stronger 'deny'.

etiam: 'even <if …>'.

crimen usually means not 'crime' but 'charge'.

primum: answered by **deinde** later.

locus: this (dangerous) place is boldly made the subject of the sentence (and described as **latronum occultator …**).

ab illo: Clodius again.

bonis: *bona* (neuter plural) can be 'goods', 'property'.

Etruria, the area to the north of Rome (now, roughly, Tuscany), was a region over which Clodius, with his private army, had established a high degree of control, fiercely resented by those who lived there.

The tenses of **sustinuisset** and **caderent** (and **citaretur**) show a slight variation; we might have expected a second pluperfect, but the switch to an imperfect gives more interest with very little difference to the meaning.

AS

Section 51

certe is emphatic and takes us back to what actually happened, rather than hypotheses: 'But in fact ...'

quod ut sciret ...: **quod** refers to the point just made, about Clodius' journey away from Rome, which is then repeated as **illum Ariciae fuisse. ut** here, picked up by **tamen**, is in the sense 'although'.

suspicari ... debuit: 'he ought to have suspected'; with 'ought' referring to the past, English puts the infinitive into the past too (taking 'ought' to be past), and does almost the same with 'could' – 'could have ...' Latin, however, uses a present infinitive and lets *debeo* or *possum* carry the past tense idea.

tangeret: subjunctive because it is in a clause inside the Indirect Statement.

deversurum <*esse*>.

ante is stressed.

Section 52

adhuc: 'up until now', 'so far'.

illi: '<whereas> to Clodius...' At almost all points from now on in this section, Cicero distinguishes between Milo and Clodius by using *hic* and *ille* rather than their names.

acerbissimum, nullum ...: both with **odium**, and adjacent to strengthen the extreme contrast.

tantum in repellenda: **tantum** in its very common meaning of 'only' (= 'only so much').

repellenda parallel with **inferenda** and both going with **vi**.

profectionis . . .: the contrasts here are between (i) **huius** and **illi**, and (ii) **profectionis** and **reditūs** (which is therefore genitive; both go with **diem**).

potius: 'more/rather', 'by contrast'.

alienum has to be an opposite of **necessarium** – 'irrelevant'.

nullius rei: the genitive is attached rather loosely to **consilium**; what is important is that it is early and emphatic, 'in no detail'.

noctem . . . exspectandam: 'night would have been to-be-waited for' = 'he would have had to wait for nightfall'. **metuendum** similarly.

AS

Section 53

caput: 'the most important point'.

locus . . . ille ipse is really the subject of the question **utri . . .** , and has been lifted out of the clause to give this key idea greater prominence (as do the surrounding pronouns **ille** and **ipse**). A more standard (and less effective) word-order would have been *utri, tandem, ille locus ipse aptior ad insidias fuerit*.

tandem = 'I ask you' (this sense has been met already, near the end of §35).

etiam = 'still' (of time).

ante fundum Clodi . . .: Cicero answers his question with another question, asking his audience to choose between a very unlikely and much more likely possibility.

hominum mille: the 'text book rules' say that whereas *milia* must take the genitive (*duo milia hominum* for 'two thousand men'), *mille* is a straightforward adjective and just goes alongside its noun (*mille homines*, if nominative); in fact expressions like **hominum mille**, with *mille* behaving as though it is a noun like *milia*, are found occasionally. So the verb **versabatur** is singular, because the subject is (a single) thousand.

versabatur: *versor* ('frequentative' of *verto*) is one of Latin's vague and versatile words, like *res*, *ago* and *gero*. Literally 'to turn oneself around in . . .', it comes to mean 'to be involved in', 'pass one's time in'; here 'were employed'.

edito . . . loco: probably a 'descriptive' ablative phrase, almost an ablative absolute with 'being' understood; 'when his opponent's position was . . .' **fore**: the alternative form for *futurus esse*, the future infinitive of *sum*.

et ob eam rem . . .: the question continues.

an in eo loco …: the question now hinges on **an**, introducing the second, and far more likely, alternative.

est … exspectatus = *exspectatus est*.

ipsius loci spe: 'the hope of …' = 'the possibilities of …'.

cogitarat = *cogitaverat* (a regular contraction for first conjugation verbs). Here *cogito* is used in a different sense from that in line 3 and means 'to plot'.

Section 54

audiretis … videretis … appareret: all *imperfect* subjunctives, 'if you were hearing (now)'.

nihil mali: 'nothing (of) wrong'; genitives are usual with 'quantity' words like *multum*; **nihil** counts as a 'quantity' word.

alter: 'one of them' – *alter* ('the other') is used to refer to either of two people.

paenulatus: in §28 Milo, who was wearing a heavy cloak (*paenula*) at the time of the encounter, was also described by this striking word **paenulatus**.

unā: 'with him' (an adverb from *unus*).

quid non impeditissimum …?: *impeditus* here, strictly passive (literally 'what was less so very encumbered?'), is better translated as though active, 'restrictive' (*impeditus* was used loosely in this way in §28, which this section deliberately recalls; in the next line it has its usual passive meaning).

vestitus: a noun (it includes Milo's *paenula*).

illum: throughout the speech, Cicero consistently uses *ille* to refer to Clodius and *hic* for Milo.

A
Level

primum: 'the first time' (Clodius returned from this trip and later made a second departure, to Rome, meeting Milo on the way).

egredientem e villa, subito: cur? vesperi: quid necesse est? tarde: qui convenit: praesertim id temporis? The **cur?** is enquiring about **subito**, and **quid necesse est?** refers to **vesperi** (why so urgent, when it was already evening?); and **qui convenit?** (**qui** = 'in what way?') is a question about **tarde** (surely he should have been getting a move on?).

Alsiensi: 'his estate in Alsium'; Alsium was an attractive spot, northwards from Rome along the coast – lying in completely the opposite direction from the area under discussion here.

perspiceret: *per-* intensifies, 'to have a good look at'.

dum hic veniret: when someone is waiting for something to happen, something he wants to happen, *dum* with the subjunctive is usual (the subjunctive giving the idea of purpose) – 'until'.

Section 55

ille refers, as usual, to Clodius.

cum uxore: '<had travelled> with ...'

castra Etrusca: there have been earlier references to this area north of Rome as being Clodius' base, e.g. §26.

comites Graeculi ... properabat: understand 'went with him' as a verb here; **tum ...** 'but on this occasion there were...' Take **nugarum** with **nihil** ('quantity' words, even **nihil**, take a genitive).

Milo qui numquam ...: '<had> never <done any such thing before> ....'

scorta: it is not clear what the difference is, if any, between **scorta** and **lupas**, and it does not particularly matter, either. Although *scortum* sometimes in Cicero means a male prostitute, if it is felt necessary that each of the three words should bear a different meaning, it may be that **scorta** is meant as a general label that would apply to both sexes.

tum neminem <*ducebat*>.

nisi ut . . .: 'except for you to say. . .', 'unless we are to suppose. . .'.

virum a viro lectum: this is a sarcastic remark – all the sharper for coming very unexpectedly. In origin, it is a military expression, the idea being that squads for particular tasks were sometimes made up by a procedure a little like what we know as 'picking teams'; but instead of team captains picking the entire team, one man picked another, who picked another, and so on. So in the literal sense, this might indeed be the way in which Clodius' 'force' had been put together. But in the context of *scorta*, *exoleti* and *lupae*, the innocent enough phrase immediately takes on overtones of a homosexual entourage – on this occasion, men picked their favourite men as a substitute for not being allowed to take women with them.

non semper . . .: in English, we might want to preserve the word-order by translating 'it does not always happen that . . .' **semper** and **nonnumquam** govern their whole clause, and the verb **occiditur** goes with both.

quia, quamquam . . .: a second reason.

imparatos: that Milo and his entourage were not prepared for the attack is an important part of Cicero's defence.

mulier inciderat in viros: another sarcastic dig. This is perhaps meant to remind the audience of the *Bona Dea* scandal of 62 BC, when Clodius disguised himself as a woman in order to take part in an all-female religious ceremony (see the online notes for §46). Here, though, the joke would be describing that situation in reverse – a *woman* finding herself in a group of *men*.

A
Level

Section 56

. . . sic . . . points forward to **ut non . . .** , a Result Clause (the negative in these is always *non*, not *ne*). **non paratus** = *imparatus*. In reading this sentence, stress **satis** (**fere** has very little meaning, and functions chiefly to put stress on *satis*; but translate the two words as 'quite sufficiently <prepared>'). Cicero is making the point that Milo was never completely unprepared against an attack by Clodius, which allows him to repeat briefly some of the reasons he has already given for why an attack was always possible.

interesset: the construction of *interest* with the genitive was more fully explained in the notes on §34. Here, 'what mattered' is expressed by a noun-clause in the accusative + infinitive (**se interire**) and then two Indirect Questions.

odio esset: a 'predicative dative' expression, 'to be hateful to/hated by'; **illi** is the dative of the person to whom he was hateful/by whom he was hated (predicative dative expressions – *bono esse, auxilio esse, odio esse* etc. – normally do have datives of the person attaching to them); **quanto** goes with **odio**.

quantum . . . auderet: 'how much he dared', i.e. 'how reckless he was'. Sometimes *possum* is used in a similar way, not with an infinitive but with an adverb, to mean 'to have strength'.

propositam et paene addictam: Cicero imagines Milo's life as in effect 'sold to the highest bidder': some 'hit-man' is bound to realize that Clodius would reward him well for liquidating Milo.

adde . .: 'add', i.e. 'we must not forget'. *adde* is common in this sense, which is why it can remain singular despite being addressed to an audience.

Martem: the personification of various aspects of war or battle as 'Mars' is quite common, even in prose writers; *ancipite Marte* is a regular way of saying that a battle finished 'indecisively'. So Cicero is not making any sort of religious statement here, but just describing what can happen to any of us (**communem**) when a conflict occurs.

evertit et perculit ...: the picture seems to be of a man gloating astride his stricken foe, but being himself killed as he is attacked in his very moment of triumph.

desperantes agrees with **quos**. Take **cum incidisset** after **quos**.

Section 57

manu misit: regarded as a single idea, to 'free' a slave 'from one's control' (*manu*), though the words can be separated (*manu vero cur miserit* below).

scilicet: a sarcastic 'obviously', as he presents an idea which he will ridicule in the rest of the section.

quid opus est tortore?: *opus est* means 'there is need of' and takes an ablative of what is needed; so **quid opus est ...?** = 'what need is there ...?', 'what is the point of having ...?'.

quid quaeris?: 'what question are you asking?' Cicero is trying to show that the torturing of the slaves, which Milo pre-empted by freeing them, would have posed no threat to him as the purpose of torturing slaves before a trial is actually quite limited.

occideritne: perfect subjunctive, because this is an abbreviated version of the Indirect Question <perhaps you want to know> *num occiderit eum?* Then Cicero answers his own question with **occidit**.

iure (ablative of *ius*) can function as an adverb, 'justifiably'. **iniuria** (also an ablative of the noun) is its opposite.

nihil ad tortorem: a verb like *pertinet* could be imagined to complete the sense ('it has nothing to do with the torturer'), but in fact expressions involving this use of *ad* often are condensed like this.

A Level

facti: 'of the deed/act', contrasting with **iuris**, 'of the justification/legality'.

quod (each time) is picked up by **id**, 'the area which . . .'

vis here from *volo*.

manu vero cur miserit . . .: a slightly obscure sentence. Cicero sets out the basic issue ('But as to why . . .') and then breaks off with **si id potius quaeris** (**id** referring to that question, which in Cicero's view is the wrong one to be asking). The singular 'you' of **quaeris** (as with **quid quaeris?**) refers either to the prosecutor or to an imaginary objector, more likely the former (not to the whole jury), and this opponent remains the subject of **nescis inimici factum reprehendere** = 'you do not know <how> to find fault with the action of an enemy', 'you are missing a chance to criticize your enemy's conduct'.

Section 58

qui semper . . . fortiter: understand <*dicit*>. **huius** refers to Cato himself. Cato was a prominent politician and a member of the jury. For more detail about him, see the notes on §44.

caput has the sense of 'life' (we talk about 'capital punishment').

defendissent: subjunctive both because the clause is still an integral part of what Cato is reported to have said and because *qui, quae, quod* with a subjunctive can suggest a reason – in this case, the reason for these rewards to be given.

quod . . . praemium: *quod* not *quid*, because when 'who/what?' is a pronoun, it is part of *quis, quis, quid*, but when it is an adjective (as here, 'what reward') it is part of *qui, quae, quod*.

etsi is just a conjunction (= ' however').

id refers to **vivit**, the fact that he is alive.

non tanti est quam ...: 'is not worth so much as ...'. *tanti* is the 'genitive of price'.

quod propter ...: quod = 'the fact that'.

dedendi is a gerundive from *dedo*, 'are to be surrendered'.

defensores necis: English uses the pattern 'defenders against his being killed', but Latin regularly uses the genitive case to link two nouns.

nihil habet ... quod minus moleste ferat: 'nothing such that he may regret it less', 'nothing for him to regret less ...', a form of Result Clause.

ipsi is the dative singular of *ipse*, contrasting with **illis**.

esse goes with **persolutum** for *persolutum esse*; the accusative + infinitive clause stands like a noun, 'the fact that he has ...'.

Section 59

quaestiones: Cicero has been talking about the desire of his opponents to have *Milo's* slaves interrogated under torture, which never happened because Milo had freed them; he now turns to interrogations that were taking place, of *Clodius'* slaves.

quibusnam: the *–nam* suffix gives a 'who on earth?' flavour to the question – 'Slaves? What slaves?' Here it suggests that this comes as news to the imagined questioner.

de Publi Clodi: understand <*servis*>.

Appius: Appius Claudius, the elder (probably) of Publius Clodius' two nephews, sons of his brother Gaius. Appius had demanded these slaves be interrogated (**postulavit**) and it had not been difficult for him to produce them (**produxit**) as they had passed into his ownership after Clodius' death.

proxime and **propius** are the superlative and comparative of *prope* and so **proxime** can take the accusative (**deos**) that *prope* takes. This, however, is a rare construction.

Because torture of a master's slaves was only allowed when some religious offence had been committed, Cicero is able to say that Clodius is being treated like a god – and then delights in reminding his audience, yet again, of Clodius' intrusion into the *Bona Dea* ceremonies ten years before (see the online notes for §46).

quaeritur is here an 'impersonal passive', 'an inquiry is being held'.

sed tamen is a particularly strong 'but'.

in dominum: *in* (+ accusative) can have the sense of 'against'.

quaeri is, again, impersonal, like **quaeritur** above; here it is the present infinitive.

non quia . . .: Cicero says that there is nothing wrong with torturing a master's slaves simply as a means of getting to the truth, but there is more to it than that; it is **indignum**, 'inappropriate' to his status; it is an extreme insult when the state interferes with what is his own property.

dominis is dative.

morte ipsa tristius: the humiliation is 'a more grim prospect' (**tristius**) than the punishment the master might face as a result of the slaves' evidence. The death penalty was in fact rare in the political trials we know about in the Roman Republic; the usual ultimate punishment was exile, and because it would finish a man's political career exile was sometimes spoken of as equivalent to death.

Section 60

Having said that torturing the slaves is no way to arrive at the truth, Cicero now pours scorn on the interrogation, imagining how a typical examination will have proceeded. He slips into colloquialisms to make the scene more lifelike – **sis** = *si vis* ('please'); **heus** is completely out of place in the normally elevated style of a speech, and Cicero does not use the word anywhere else in his speeches ('Oi, you!').

verbi causa: he has picked a typical name for a slave, 'to give him a name'.

mentiare: an alternative spelling for *mentiaris*, present subjunctive of *mentior*, because **cave** introduced an Indirect Command, with *ne* understood (another colloquialism) – 'Be careful you don't . . .).

The result of giving the wrong answer will be **certa crux**.

quid . . . certius?: 'what is more reliable . . .?'

The way this examination was conducted is now contrasted with the normal way of doing it. **ceteri** are kept away from contact with the outside world, so that no-one can talk to them and interfere with the course of justice (perhaps by threatening them); but Clodius' slaves (**hi**, heavily emphasized by its position) spent a lengthy period under the complete control (**penes** is a strong word) of the prosecutor, Appius Claudius, one of the nephews of the dead man.

cum has been delayed to give more prominence to the irregularity Cicero is highlighting. In translation, it has to come at the beginning of the clause.

Section 61

quod si: 'but if'.

cum . . .: 'although . . . .'.

tam claris . . .: inserting *tam* in an arrangement like this is simply an idiom and it is probably unnecessary to translate the word. It is

A
Level

normal to add *tam* when an adjective with a noun is preceded by a demonstrative adjective (as in *haec tam pulchra urbs*) or sometimes, as here, by a 'quantity' word.

pura ... revertisse is the Indirect Statement following **cernitis**. What is important is not **Romam revertisse** – we know that Milo returned – but the elaborate insistence of Cicero that he did so with an entirely clear conscience.

recordamini is the imperative (of a deponent verb), and is the main verb (the **quod si ...** clause has finished).

reditus is genitive; **eius** is not to be taken in agreement with it, but just means 'his'; **ingressus** is a noun, not the participle.

qui ... rather than *quis*, as here **qui** (and **quae**) are adjectives going with the nouns (**celeritas, ingressus** and **oratio**). Interrogative 'what ...' is *quis, quis, quid* if it is a pronoun, but *qui, quae, quod* if it is an adjective going with a noun. The same distinction operates with *aliquis* and *aliqui*.

oratio: Milo delivered a speech on his return.

neque vero ... commisit ...: Milo 'entrusted himself to' the people, the Senate etc. simply by returning; he could have remained in a self-imposed exile, for his own safety, but trusted them, if he did return to Rome, not to surrender him to the forces that Clodius had represented.

eius ...: Cicero now begins to speak about Pompey (it is more impressive not to name him). Pompey occupied a unique constitutional position in Rome's crisis at this time, being consul without a colleague and having enormous powers, which Cicero here describes in a general way.

cui numquam ...: cui is simply a link with the previous sentence (a 'connecting relative'); it is better translated as 'to him' than 'to whom'.

causae: 'cause' in the sense used in 'championing a cause'.

audienti ... metuenti ... suspicanti ... credenti are participles agreeing with **cui;** the sentence began **cui** (= Pompey) **numquam se ... tradidisset;** Cicero begins to explain why Milo might have had reservations about trusting Pompey, as he was 'a man who was told everything ...', much of which might be just rumour that could have damaged Milo; nonetheless, so confident was he that he returned.

in utramque partem: 'in both directions' (a quite common meaning of *pars*).

ut neque timeant qui ...: **qui** = *ei qui*.

versari: this vague word occurs again. We would say the punishment 'plays' or 'is dangled' before their eyes.

Section 62

certa with **ratione**, not **causa; ratione certa** is the key idea and is being emphasized here.

causa: 'cause', as above.

facti is here a noun (*factum* a 'deed'). In **facti rationem, praesentiam animi, defensionis constantiam,** Cicero is using a characteristic arrangement of three elements (a 'tricolon'), but for more than just the rhetorical effect; he actually refers to three different aspects of Milo's behaviour – that the killing of Clodius had an acceptable explanation (*facti rationem*), that Milo had acted quickly and with much self-control in returning to Rome and seizing the initiative (*praesentiam animi*), and (in *defensionis constantiam*) that he had remained unrepentant about what had happened.

A
Level

obliti estis . . .: *obliviscor*, which is generally followed by a genitive (except when only a vague neuter word is its object), here has accusative objects (**sermones et opiniones**). Perhaps a reason is that if genitives were used here, the resulting pile-up of genitives would make the sentence too hard to follow.

nuntio: *nuntius* here must be 'message', 'report', not 'messenger'.

imperitorum: *imperitus* is usually simply the opposite of *peritus* ('skilled', 'experienced'); but here the 'inexperienced', contrasted with **inimicorum**, are the 'don't knows', those who have not made their minds up about Milo, though Clark takes the word to mean 'undiscerning'.

negabant . . .: *nego* is generally used in an Indirect Statement in preference to *dico . . . non . . .* It is like, in English, saying not 'I think he will not return', but 'I *don't think* he will return' – Latin shows in other ways a preference for bringing a negative word to the start of a sentence.

Section 63

sive . . .: normally, we find two *sive* clauses within the same sentence, giving alternative possibilities ('Whether X, or whether Y, still . . .'). Here, the two possibilities are spread over two different sentences. 'Whether . . .' will not work; it will be better to translate them as 'If, on the one hand . . .' and 'If, on the other hand . . .' The subjunctives (**fecisset, voluisset, servasset**) are used because these 'if . . .' clauses are part of the Indirect Statement after **arbitrabantur**.

ut . . .: strictly, a Result Clause follows *ut* ('with the result that he . . .'); but it just means 'in the sense that . . .', explaining *animo irato ac percito* by *incensus odio*.

tanti ... ut ...: **tanti** is a 'genitive of price' (or 'value') leading to the Result Clause beginning at **ut**, 'important enough for him to say goodbye to ...'.

explesset for *explevisset*; the *–vi-* syllable has dropped out, just as it often does with regular First Conjugation verbs – *portasset* for *portavisset* etc.

etiam: 'actually' (a suggestion Cicero does not in fact accept, but others inevitably considered it).

non dubitaturum: understand <*arbitrabantur*>.

quin: not such a troublesome word as textbooks often try to suggest. *non dubito quin* (+ subjunctive) – notice the 'hesitating' must be made negative for *quin* to be used – is a way of saying 'I do not hesitate to ...', i.e. 'I do <something> without hesitation' (though *dubito* + infinitive is more common). A clue to understanding *quin* is that generally it is followed by something that did or probably will happen – it has a positive colouring.

fortem virum gives the reason he will not hesitate to take what is coming to him.

suo periculo: 'at personal risk/cost', an 'ablative of attendant circumstances', or perhaps of instrument ('by ... ').

haec: all that life in Rome means to them.

fruenda: the gerundive of *fruor* agreeing with **haec**, 'to be enjoyed', 'for you to enjoy'. Although deponent verbs like *fruor* are supposed to have no passive forms, several of them do use gerundives, which are passive in meaning; so *sequendus* means 'to be followed/being followed'. Furthermore, *fruor* is a verb that takes the ablative, but this is still not a barrier to the use of a passive part of the grammar as the meaning is so immediate and obvious.

A
Level

servasset: the (pluperfect) subjunctive because the idea is still part of what the people in Rome thought (*arbitrabantur . . .*); he had saved what he was leaving behind, but they could still enjoy it.

illa: from the past – though only in fact from 63/62 BC, just ten years before; but the memory went deep into Roman consciousness.

erumpet: Catiline, declared an enemy of the state, set up a camp in northern Italy and fought against the troops sent from Rome to suppress him. **erumpet** (future tense) is vague, but seems to mean that Milo, like Catiline, will show his true colours and launch armed opposition to Rome.

miseros . . .: an 'accusative of exclamation'. Cicero is making a comment about people like Milo (and himself), whose services to the state are so conveniently forgotten by so many of their fellow-citizens. He is not addressing remarks *to* them, for which the vocative case would be used (cf. *o me miserum*, 'unhappy me').

optime de ... meritos: *bene meritus sum de X* means literally 'I have deserved well from X', but it is only true that you really do deserve well of somebody if you have first done something to deserve it, and so the expression is a common one in effect meaning 'I have served X well'.

in quibus: **in** means 'in the case of'.

obliviscuntur is again (cf. §62) used with an ordinary accusative object, instead of the genitive which it more regularly takes. The reason here, if there needs to be one, is that using the genitive would fail to produce the pointed contrast between *praeclarissimas* and *nefarias*, as different cases would be being used and *res* would have to be used twice. Latin also has an aversion to piling up genitive plurals especially when this would produce a string of heavy *-orum –arum* endings; so *causa* ('for the sake of') generally takes a gerund rather than a plural gerundive expression – e.g. *statuas videndi causa* rather than *statuarum videndarum causa*.

Section 64

exstitissent: *exsisto* is sometimes used as a stronger word for 'to be'; the accusations made against Milo 'would have turned out to be' true.

admisisset: *admitto*, like *committo*, can be used by itself to mean 'commit a crime'.

Sections 64–71

Cicero refers to a number of wild accusations made against Milo – that he had stashed weapons away in secret places and even planned to assassinate Pompey. He praises both Milo and Pompey for their careful responses to these rumours, which were investigated and found groundless.

Section 72

crimen: always take care with this word. In this section it has its usual meaning, 'charge, accusation'.

vestri sensus: genitive with the adjectives **ignarus** and **expers**.

ita ... ut ...: 'in the way that I have ...', i.e. by arguing that Milo was innocent and Clodius the one who plotted to commit a murder; *not* arguing that the death of Clodius was a good thing anyway.

A
Level

Spurium Maelium: Spurius Maelius is a figure from earlier Roman history, as was Tiberius Gracchus (see the later notes on this section for more about both of them).

annona ... iacturisque : 'by ...', ablatives of cause.

iacturisque: *iactura-ae* (feminine) is a noun, meaning 'loss' or 'waste' or, as here, 'expenditure'.

regni appetendi: with *suspicionem*.

conlegae seems to be a simple genitive, though Poynton says it is a dative, in the sense of '<removed> from' (sometimes called the 'dative of disadvantage'). The man referred to, elected with Gracchus (**conlegae**) as one of the ten tribunes for 133 BC, was Marcus Octavius. Here, **magistratum** is the 'magistracy' or 'office', not the 'magistrate' who holds it.

per seditionem: phrases with *per* are often just adverbial; Cicero means that Gracchus was acting provocatively.

implerunt = *impleverunt*.

auderet: Milo is the subject. Some strong claims are to follow, hence **auderet**.

periculo suo: 'at such danger/possible cost to himself'; ablative either of 'means' ('by ...') or of 'attendant circumstances' ('when there was ...'). Notice the stress on *suo*.

sed eum ...: the structure of the sentence is *occidi non Spurium Maelium ... sed eum ...* (= Clodius).

feminae: these are the women present at the *Bona Dea* rites of 62 BC, which Clodius had desecrated (see the online notes for §46). **adulterium**, because it had been alleged that he was pursuing an affair with Caesar's then wife, Pompeia.

A Level

Section 73

supplicio: ablative ('by . . .'), linking with **expiandas**.

religiones: here, 'religious ceremonies'.

expiandas: 'had to be . . .', 'could only be . . .'.

saepe: i.e. at several meetings.

comperisse: *-isse* rather than *-iisse* is very common (not least with compounds of *eo*); the contraction happens in other appropriate parts of the verb, like the pluperfect subjunctive.

eum qui civem quem . . .: slightly difficult to follow because the pattern is not the same as that of the preceding clauses; if you imagine pauses after *civem* and *iudicarant*, the relative clause 'nested' inside a relative clause is easier to accommodate.

urbis and **vitae civium** go with **conservatorem**.

iudicarant = *iudicaverant*.

exterminavit: not 'exterminated' (Cicero is here talking about himself) but 'put beyond the *terminus*', i.e. 'exiled', in 58 BC. He rarely misses the opportunity to remind audiences of his suppression of Catiline's conspiracy in 63 BC (**urbis . . . conservatorem**) though here the reference is not gratuitous, as it was precisely his actions then which became the grounds for his exile.

regna dedit seems a fanciful exaggeration, but some basis of fact lies behind it.

singulari virtute et gloria: with **civem** (an 'ablative of description', especially common for giving a person's qualities. The **civem** is Pompey, in an episode described earlier in the speech (§18).

A
Level

domum: '<to/into> his house'; *domum* does not usually take a preposition for 'to' (rather like our expression 'to go home'), and similarly *domo* without the preposition means 'from home'.

nec in facinore nec in libidine: a contrast between his actions and his wicked intentions.

aedem Nympharum: this is the equivalent of the Public Record Office. Perhaps it was the details of membership of the Senate and occupants of other state offices that were recorded (*recensio*) and displayed there on bronze tablets (*tabulae*).

Section 74

eum denique . . .: remember that *occidi* (two whole sections back) is still the verb, in this lengthy imagined claim on the lips of Milo.

denique: 'finally', not of time (not the same as *tandem*) but 'my last point', commonly used in a speech to indicate that a list (usually of vehement criticism) is nearing an end. Cicero seems to use it prematurely here.

nulla lex erat: although the translation 'for whom no law existed' makes some sense, it seems to put too much weight onto **erat** to be rhetorically effective. Granted the emphatic position of **nulla** and, in a moment, **nullum**, it seems better to take them as predicates rather than straight adjectives, i.e. equivalent to *nihil* ('meant nothing'). Or perhaps 'there was no such thing as ...', keeping the stress on the negative words.

ius is not quite the same as **lex**; here it is the word for the 'rights' an individual enjoyed. Latin does not seem to have a word for our modern concept of 'human rights', but does use *ius gentium* for what we might call 'international law', i.e. the rights to which any people or state is entitled.

A
Level

nulli: again, although Cicero might be saying 'there were no limits to his own possessions', this is not the point. The section is about Clodius' ambitions for more possessions (**spem possessionum** below). So this is better taken, parallel to the other **nullus** words here, as 'for whom boundary-marks to <other people's> possessions were an irrelevance'.

qui ... alienos fundos ... petebat, not by the more usual though disreputable routes of cheating on the legal side but by what were virtually military occupations.

calumnia litium: *calumnia* (ablative here) generally means a 'slander' (as in the English word 'calumny'). But it also has technical legal meanings and here **calumnia (litium)** is 'malicious intent (in bringing cases to court)', 'fraudulent prosecutions'.

Note that *alienus* is a quite different word from *alius*; here it has its very strict sense of 'belonging to another'. Notice also its emphatic position, in front of rather than following **fundos**.

signis are military standards: *signa infero* is a set phrase for charging forward into battle.

hunc . . . iudicem nostrum: Varius is present in court, as a member of the jury.

qui cum architectis . . .: yet another descriptive clause after *occidi eum qui . . . qui . . . qui . . .* etc.

hortos: quite often in the plural, 'gardens', so 'estate'. The *villa* is the building on such an estate, the *horti* the surrounding lands.

Ianiculo . . .: Clodius' ambition for other men's property stopped only at the Janiculum Hill (the western limit of Rome) and the Alps (the northern limit of Italy).

ab equite: the man is an 'equestrian', his rank in the social hierarchy – a man of some wealth but not a member of the Senate.

A
Level

ab equite . . . non impetrasset ut . . .: *impetro* is an idiomatic word, but not always easy to translate. Clodius had not 'gained from' this equestrian 'that he should . . .', i.e. he had not 'got his way' with him, 'been successful', in the matter of getting him to sell him this island so that he could build on it.

materiem is general, and the more specific list that follows explains it.

trans: 'on the other side of'.

non dubitavit: he 'did not hesitate' to do what he wanted. Clodius' speed of action has already been suggested by *repente*, but he did not feel the force of any legal objections either.

in alieno: neuter, 'on what was another's'.

Section 75

qui huic Tito Furfanio . . .: he breaks off, in order quickly to include two more examples of Clodius' bullying people out of their property; the sentence resumes with the words repeated and the construction slightly changed at **ausum esse Tito Furfanio dicere** . . .

quid . . . dicam: a favourite method ancient orators use for covering their material rapidly, called *paraleipsis* – 'What shall I say about . . .'; by asking the question, the orator does in fact mention the point, which is normally all he wants to do. Here Cicero adds the detail which these two victims of Clodius had in common. **dicam** may either be a future tense, or, more likely, a present subjunctive (the 'deliberative subjunctive' for 'What am I to say . . .?).

muliercula: the point of the diminutive form is to suggest how helpless she was to resist Clodius' demands; Aponius is described as **adulescente** for the same reason.

utrique: because *minor* takes the dative.

possessione: we might have expected the accusative, but the ablative makes sense too – 'to yield in the ownership of their estates'.

cessissent because Clodius' original threat would be, 'if you do not yield to me . . .', and if this were said directly in Latin, not as part of an Indirect Statement, it would involve the otherwise rare 'future perfect' tense ('if you *will* not *have yielded* . . .'). When this future perfect is absorbed into an Indirect Statement, as here, the verb must become a subjunctive, but there is no such thing as a future perfect subjunctive, so the only appropriate tense to keep the 'completion' idea of 'shall have given' is the pluperfect, in historic sequence (or the perfect subjunctive if in primary sequence).

ausum esse: if this really is what Cicero wrote, he has lost grammatical control slightly; it seems impossible to integrate this accusative + infinitive into the structure he has actually given the clause. We have to imagine he has said 'I tell you that . . .' somewhere earlier on.

dedisset is pluperfect subjunctive for the same reason as **cessissent** in the previous sentence.

mortuum is clearly being used here as a noun – 'a dead body'. By carrying out this macabre threat, Clodius would have brought a form of religious pollution on Furfanius' house. Perhaps the word reflects a colloquial usage (like the American 'stiff'), and is intended to suggest Clodius' actual words, or at least the gangster-like atmosphere in which he operated.

inlaturum: from *infero*.

**A
Level**

qua invidia . . .: a purpose clause, explaining how Clodius was relying on the fact that his victim would become such a social outcast because of the pollution in his house that that would be the end of him – he would be a 'spent force' (**conflagrandum**). The gerund implies that this outcome would have been inevitable.

The words **tali viro** are simply parallel to **huic**, and not essential to the clause, but they suggest that Furfanius could never have lived this down 'being the sort of man he was'.

vestibulum: it seems that Clodius and his sister lived in adjacent houses, sharing a courtyard at the front (**vestibulum**). Clodius selfishly adapted the boundary wall somehow so that his sister was left with no proper entrance to her property.

ducere: here, 'to extend' (or 'to build', if there was not in fact a *paries* between them before).

Section 76

Cicero has just ended the lengthy imagined defence he has put into the mouth of Milo. He now resumes speaking as himself.

The long opening sentence should be read as follows:

> **quamquam haec quidem** ('these activities of his', soon to be contrasted – *quidem* often suggests a contrast – with what he planned to do later) **iam tolerabilia videbantur**

> [harsher tone] **etsi aequabiliter in rem publicam, in privatos** (contrasting pair), **in longinquos, in propinquos** (not the usual meaning, 'relatives', but to contrast and rhyme with *longinquos*; so another contrasting pair), **in alienos** (members of other families), **in suos** (meaning his brother and sister, referred to a few lines earlier) **inruebat**

[despairing, incredulous tone] **sed nescioquo modo** ('somehow') **usu** ('with experience' – ours, who viewed all this as just about *tolerabilia*) **obduruerat et percalluerat** (synonyms for 'grow hardened to', *obduresco* and *percallesco*) **civitatis incredibilis patientia** (*patientia* is the subject of the verbs)

[now the main clause, after the 'although' beginning] **quae vero** ('as for what . . .') **aderant iam et impendebant, quonam modo** ('in what possible way') **ea aut depellere potuissetis** ('would you have been able to . . .') **aut ferre?**

omitto . . .: 'I leave out' (*paraleipsis* again, as in §75).

tetrarchas: 'rulers' (a Greek term, *tetrarches, -ae,* for one of the kings in an area constituting four (Greek *tetr-*) kingdoms).

faceretis: imperfect subjunctives are used for what would (now) be happening.

se . . . immitteret: a metaphor from horse-racing, 'let himself go' – perhaps 'let himself loose'.

possessiones are possessions in the form of land, 'property'; **tecta** 'houses/buildings'; **pecunias**, normally understood as 'money', suggests more here – 'material goods', perhaps. The plural emphasizes the threat to so many individuals.

liberis: *liberi* 'children'.

numquam is heavily emphasized.

fingi . . .: the question begins scornfully, with the first word emphatically spat out.

tenentur here for *memoria tenentur,* 'are remembered'.

servorum: the terrifying word is stressed by its position. **illum . . . conscripturum fuisse** expresses by an accusative and infinitive this fact, that is so well known and not being fabricated – that Clodius was going to use gangs of slaves to carry out wholesale confiscations of property.

conscripturum fuisse: this *-urus fuisse* form is Latin's way of expressing 'would have' as an infinitive (so *conscripsisset* has become **conscripturum fuisse**); *conscripturum esse* would just have been the ordinary future infinitive.

Section 77

clamaret: imperfect subjunctive again for what might *now* be happening.

Titus Annius: Milo's full name is Titus Annius Milo.

Adeste: *esto* and *este* are the imperatives of *sum*. *Adsum* often has overtones of 'come and help'. **quaeso** is a form of *quaero*, usually used, as here, for parentheses (i.e. where brackets or commas are used to separate the word from the sentence).

furores: plural for emphasis.

nullis iam legibus . . .: 'no longer by . . .' – Clodius was well out of control.

iudiciis: 'judgements', 'rulings' of courts.

hoc . . . hac . . . = 'my'.

per me ut unum . . .: **ut** has been delayed to give stress on **per unum** and **me**: 'with the result that by me alone . . .'.

ius = **aequitas**, **leges** = (in the sense that they are requisite for) **libertas**, and **pudor** = **pudicitia**; the effect of the paired *tricolon* is more important than any subtle distinctions in the meanings of the paired words. The effect is reinforced by marked alliteration.

maneret: use of the singular is entirely normal, despite the list of six subjects; a verb can be singular if the nearest subject is singular.

esset vero timendum . . .: *timeo* in the sense of 'be uncertain about'; the idea is sarcastic, helped by *vero* ('to be sure!').

nunc: '(even) as it is' (without Milo having made this dramatic claim).

probet: subjunctive (from *probo -are*); this will not show in translation, but the subjunctive is used because of the idiom *quis est qui*, which introduces a form of Result Clause ('who is there such that the result would be that he . . .?'). Similarly *is sum qui*, 'I am the sort of person to . . .'

unum post hominum memoriam: 'the one man in human history'.

maxima laetitia . . . adfecisse: *adficio* is used of 'affecting' people with particular emotions – 'making them feel' 'filling them with' joy, sorrow etc. Hence the ablative for **maxima laetitia**.

non queo = *nequeo* (a part that Cicero never uses), 'I am unable'.

vetera illa: i.e. in earlier Roman history, before their own lifetime.

The idiom *vetera illa . . . gaudia quanta fuerint iudicare* for *iudicare quanta vetera illa . . . gaudia fuerint iudicare*: what is really the subject of the Indirect Question has been taken outside it and made the object of the introductory verb. The effect could be kept in translation by beginning 'As to those . . . , I cannot . . .'.

tam: 'so . . .' as Milo's is.

attulit: from *adfero*.

Section 78

bona: treated as a noun ('benefits'), going with **multa**.

singulis: 'one by one', i.e. 'in each one of these . . .'.

A
Level

ita: pointing forward to what they will think, **vivo . . . visuros fuisse**.

vivo Publio Clodio: the ablative absolute represents a conditional clause, 'if Clodius . . .' Hence the **visuros fuisse** form for 'you would have seen'.

sumus adducti = *adducti sumus*, reversed to allow more emphasis on *verissimam*.

hunc ipsum annum . . . salutarem civitati fore is the hope (*spem*) they now have.

hoc summo viro consule . . .: these four ablative expressions are the reasons why it will be a good year. The *tetracolon* is marked out clearly by the three *com-/con-* compounds.

confractis: *confringo* is a stronger form of *frango*.

constitutis: *constituo* 'settle' as well as 'decide'; so '(re-)established'.

qui . . . arbitretur: subjunctive used because of the Result Clause idea, 'such that he would think', but translate naturally as 'who thinks'/'<so crazy> as to think'.

quid? = 'And here is another point.'

privata atque vestra: 'as your own personal property'.

dominante homine furioso: another 'conditional' ablative absolute.

quod ius . . .: this is actually the question. The subject of **potuissent** is 'your property', which produces a slightly odd literal meaning by which the property, rather than the owners, would have had 'what right of perpetual possession?'

habere potuissent: *possum* takes a present infinitive, unlike the English pattern 'could have had'.

odio inimicitiarum mearum: the genitive means 'to do with', 'arising from'.

A
Level

libentius ... quam verius: there are two comparatives (adverbs), whereas in English we should only expect one, but this is the normal Latin idiom ('with more pleasure (rather) than (more) truth').

evomere (*evomo -ere -vomui -vomitum*) is a strong word – 'to spew all this out', 'to vent my spleen', 'to discharge this torrent of words'.

etenim illustrates or (as here) explains a point just made – 'the truth is that ...'.

praecipuum: 'special (to me)', referring to the *odium*. Cicero had a long list of reasons to hate Clodius, principally Clodius' engineering his exile six years previously.

aequaliter versaretur odium meum: *versor* is a very vague word, so that *aequaliter versaretur* is equivalent to *aequalis* (= *aequus*) *esset* ('operates at the same level', more literally).

ne cogitari quidem: 'not even to be imagined'.

exiti is for *exitii* (the genitive of *-ium* and *-ius* nouns is shortened by Cicero).

quantum ... sceleris/exiti: 'much' with a *singular* noun is in Latin *multum* (neuter) + genitive (*multum pecuniae*, 'much money'). The same usage is observed with 'more', 'most', 'so much', 'how much' (*plus, plurimum, tantum, quantum*) and equivalent words (*aliquantum timoris*, 'some fear').

Section 79

quin ('why do you not ...?') with an imperative is unusual in Cicero; it seems to be conversational, with a flavour of 'you really should listen to me'.

A
Level

cernamus ... videmus: these verbs are often found together, sometimes with a distinction in meaning (*cerno* as 'see clearly'), but here they just seem to be synonyms.

huius condicionis meae: 'this my situation', which he then explains as **si possim ...**

si is occasionally used, rather than *num*, to introduce an Indirect Question (as is 'if' in English) – '<to see> if I can ...'.

Milonem ut absolvatis: **ut** is delayed, perhaps another conversational touch.

sed ita: 'but <look at it> in this way'.

vivus: '<if he were> living'.

The **cogitatione** is **inani** because it has no basis, is 'imaginary'.

quid?: as in §78.

ea virtute et fortuna: ablatives of description, '<a man of> ...'.

With **potuerit** understand *facere*.

illum clearly refers to Pompey; Cicero could, and by the rules possibly should, have written *praeter se*, but **illum** is perfectly clear.

facturum fuisse: 'would have done'.

ultores: ironic. In a sense, the jurors are being asked to 'avenge' Clodius' death, but few of them, Cicero thinks, would really see themselves in that light.

si putetis ... nolitis: an unusual combination of subjunctive and indicative in a conditional, though Tacitus and other later writers sometimes use this for effect. It is difficult to reproduce this effect, of imagination being bluntly replaced by reality, in translation; perhaps 'if you found yourselves thinking ..., you actually do not want this.'

huius clearly refers to Clodius, even though almost everywhere else in the speech he is *ille* (as twice already in this section). But as the pronoun is picking up a reference in the previous sentence, part of *hic* is much more natural.

Imagine a slight break before **ab eisne**; his question starts here.

Section 80

quae res divinas . . .: vidi is still the verb. These are 'religious activities', solemn ceremonies and commemorations still observed.

talibus . . . viris: dative.

quos cantus, quae carmina: these are probably meant as virtual synonyms, but if there is a difference, **cantus** are tunes and **carmina** the words; perhaps there is a wider distinction between 'songs' and 'poems'.

prope ad immortalitatis et religionem et memoriam consecrantur: a sonorous but rather obscure statement; these heroes are sanctified to/to have (**ad**) a 'religious status/holiness' (**religionem**) and memory 'of/characterized by immortality' (**immortalitatis**); the genitive is equivalent to an adjective ('which will last for ever'). **prope** and *paene* are regularly used by orators apparently to soften an extreme statement; what these little words do is in fact to draw attention to the huge claim being made, and in effect strengthen it.

sceleris is 'wickedness' rather than a specific 'crime' (as none is under discussion at this point).

The future tense **adficietis** alerts us to the fact that this is going to be a question.

magno animo: 'wholeheartedly'.

quod: 'something which'.

vere: not *vero* or *verum* but equivalent to *iure*, 'with truth', 'with justification'.

A
Level

Section 81–105

In the remainder of the speech – the last quarter – Cicero continues to claim that the death of Clodius was a supreme blessing to Rome; he suggests that the gods themselves had a hand in engineering it.

He portrays Milo presenting a brave and unemotional argument to the court that they should spare him from a guilty verdict leading to his exile, when his whole life has been directed towards serving the Roman people. Cicero pleads with the jury, begging them to realize the tremendous harm they will be inflicting on themselves if they convict Milo.

Vocabulary

Names of people and places are usually only given if they occur in an adjectival form (e.g. *Clodianus*).

Perfect tenses ending *-ivi* are often shortened to *-ii*.

The gender indication (c) (= 'common') means that the word can be either masculine or feminine.

An asterisk by a word indicates that it is included in OCR's Defined Vocabulary List for AS.

*a, ab (+ abl)	from; by
abicio -ere -ieci -iectum	I throw down
abiectus -a -um	desperate, pathetic
abrogo -are -avi -atum	I vote down, cancel, remove
absens absentis	absent
absolvo -ere absolvi absolutum	I acquit
*ac, atque	and
accedo -ere accessi accessum	I approach
accessus -ūs (m)	approach
*accidit -ere accidit	it happens
accusator -oris (m)	prosecutor
*acer acris acre	keen, vigorous
acerbus -a -um	bitter
*ad (+ acc)	to; for; relevant to, to do with; near
addictus -a -um	auctioned off
*addo -ere addidi additum	I add
adduco -ere adduxi adductum	I bring
adfero adferre attuli allatum	I bring

adficio -ere adfeci adfectum	I affect, move, fill (with a feeling), decorate
***adhuc**	so far, up to now
***adimo -ere ademi ademptum**	I take away
***adipiscor -i adeptus**	I obtain, gain
aditus -ūs (m)	approach
***adiuvo -are adiuvi adiutum**	I help
admitto -ere -misi -missum	I commit (a crime)
adorior -iri adortus	I attack
adripio -ere adripui adreptum	I snatch away
adsequor -i adsecutus	I gain
***adsum adesse adfui**	I am present
***adulescens adulescentis** (m)	young man
adulterium -ii (n)	adultery
adventus -ūs (m)	arrival
***adversus -a -um**	facing
aedes aedis (f)	temple
***aedificium -ii** (n)	building
aequabiliter	equally
aequaliter	equally
aequitas -tatis (f)	fairness, just dealing
***aequus -a -um**	equal, fair
aequo animo	calmly
aetas aetatis (f)	age, period
***ago agere ēgi actum**	I do; I act, behave; I make
age	come now
agrestis -e	from the countryside; rough
Albanum -i (n)	estate at Alba
alienus -a -um	someone else's; irrelevant, pointless
aliqui -qua -quod	some (*adj*)
***aliquis aliquis aliquid**	someone, something (*pronoun*)

*alius alia aliud	other
Alsiensis -e	in Alsium
*alter altera alterum	the other, the one (of two)
amicitia -ae (f)	friendship
*amicus -i (m)	friend
amitto -ere amisi amissum	I lose
amplector -i amplexus	I embrace
amplus -a -um	large, generous
amplius	more (*adj*)
*an	or (*in a question*)
*ancilla -ae (f)	female servant, maid
anima -ae (f)	breath, life
*animus -i (m)	mind, spirit, attitude
annona -ae (f)	corn supply
*annus -i (m)	year
*ante (+ acc)	before; in front of;
	(*as advb*) previously
*antea	previously
anteverto -ere -verti -versum	I anticipate, get ahead of
*aperio -ire aperui apertum	I open, reveal
apertus -a -um	open
*appareo -ēre	I appear, become clear
apparo -are –avi -atum	I prepare, plan
appello -are -avi -atum	I call (on)
appeto -ere -ii -itum	I seek
Appius -a -um	(built by) Appius, Appian
appropero -are -avi -atum	I hurry
*appropinquo -are -avi -atum (+ dat)	I approach
aptus -a -um	suitable
*apud (+ acc)	among, with
arbitror -ari arbitratus	I think

arca arcae (f)	cell
architectus -i (m)	architect
ardeo -ēre arsi arsum	I burn
argumentor -ari -atus	I argue
argumentum -i (n)	argument, proof
***arma -orum** (n) (pl)	arms, weapons; equipment; power
***at**	but
***atque**	= **ac**
atqui	but
atrium -ii (n)	hall
attendo -ere attendi attentum	I give attention
attuli	*see* **adfero**
auctoritas -tatis (f)	authority
audacia -ae (f)	daring; recklessness
***audax audacis**	bold, reckless
***audeo -ēre ausus**	I dare
***audio -ire -ivi -itum**	I hear
***aufero auferre abstuli ablatum**	I take away
***augeo -ēre auxi auctum**	I increase
augustus -a -um	solemn
auspicium -ii (n)	omen, (taking of) auspices
***aut**	or
***aut … aut …**	either … or …
***autem**	however; moreover
barbarus -a -um	barbarian, foreign; savage
***bellum -i** (n)	war
belua -ae (f)	wild animal, monster
***beneficium -ii** (n)	benefit, favour
benevolus -a -um	well-disposed, devoted
***bonus -a -um**	good

*bona -orum (n) (pl)	goods, property
bono est	it is good (for), advantageous (to)
*cado -ere cecidi casum	I fall; I fall out of sight, disappear
caecus -a -um	blind
*caedes caedis (f)	killing, murder
caedo -ere cecidi caesum	I kill
caementum -i (n)	rough stone
caerimonia -ae (f)	(religious) ceremony
calceus -i (m)	shoe
calumnia -ae (f)	malicious accusation
calx calcis (f)	limestone, lime
*campus -i (m)	field
Campus -i (m)	the Campus Martius, where voting took place
cantus -ūs (m)	song, hymn
*caput capitis (n)	head; life; origin; main point
careo -ēre -ui -itum (+ abl)	I lack, live without
carmen carminis (n)	song, poem
Cassianus -a -um	of Cassius
*castra -orum (n pl)	(military) camp
casus -ūs (m)	happening, accident
casu	by chance, as it happens
*causa -ae (f)	cause, reason; (legal) case
*causa (after gen)	for the sake of; so as to
*caveo -ēre cavi cautum	I am careful (not to . . .)
*cedo -ere cessi cessum (+ dat)	I yield to
celeritas -tatis (f)	speed
censeo -ēre censui censum	I propose, pronounce
centum	hundred
centuria -ae (f)	century (a voting unit)

cerno -ere crevi cretum	I see
certe	certainly
***certus -a -um**	certain, definite
cervix cervicis (f)	neck
***ceteri -ae -a**	the other(s)
cito -are -avi -atum	I summon
civilis -e	(typical) of a citizen; among citizens
***civis civis** (c)	citizen
***civitas -tatis** (f)	state
***clamo -are -avi -atum**	I shout
***clamor -oris** (m)	shout
***clarus -a -um**	clear, bright; famous
Clodianus -a -um	of Clodius, relating to Clodius
***coepi coeptum**	I began
cogitatio -ionis (f)	thought
***cogito -are -avi -atum**	I think (about), imagine; I plan
***cogo -ere coegi coactum**	I force
cohibeo -ēre -ui -itum	I control, keep away
Collinus -a -um	Colline (name of a voting tribe)
colloco -are -avi -atum	I place, set
***comes comitis** (c)	companion, fellow-traveller
comitatus -ūs (m)	retinue, entourage
comitia -orum (n) (pl)	election
***committo -ere -misi -missum**	I entrust; I commit a crime
commoror -ari -atus	I wait
communis -e	common, shared
***comparo -are -avi -atum**	I compare; I get ready
compello -ere -puli -pulsum	I drive
comperio -ire comperii compertum	I find out
competitor -oris (m)	rival, fellow-candidate

complures -a	several
comprehendo -ere -di -sum	I seize, catch, discover
comprimo -ere -pressi -pressum	I restrain
conatus -ūs (m)	attempt
concedo -ere -cessi -cessum	I allow, grant
concito -are -avi -atum	I arouse, arrange
concupisco -ere -cupii -cupitum	I long for
condicio -ionis (f)	condition, terms
***confero -ferre -tuli -latum**	I bring, take
se conferre	to take oneself (to), to go (to)
***conficio -ere -feci -fectum**	I finish; I establish
***confido -ere confisus** (+ dat)	I trust, believe in, am confident
confiteor -ēri confessus	I confess
conflagro -are -avi -atum	I burn up, am ruined
confringo -ere -fregi -fractum	I break, destroy
congredior -i congressus	I meet
conicio -ere -ieci -iectum	I throw, hurl
coniunctus -a -um	joined
***coniunx coniugis** (c)	wife, husband
coniveo -ēre conivi	I condone, turn a blind eye
conlega -ae (m)	colleague, fellow magistrate
conloquor -i -locutus	I talk with
***conor -ari conatus**	I try
conroboratus -a -um	strengthened
conscientia -ae (f)	conscience, guilt
conscribo -ere -scripsi -scriptum	I enrol
consecro -are -avi -atum	I consecrate
consensus -ūs (m)	agreement, support
consequor -i consecutus	I gain

conservator -oris (m)	saviour
***consilium -ii** (n)	plan, intention
constanter	with determination
constantia -ae (f)	determination
***constituo -ere constitui constitutum**	I establish, settle; I decide
consto -are -stiti -statum	I stand together, am consistent, agree
constat	it is agreed
constringo -ere -strinxi -strictum	I restrain, neutralise, crush
consuetudo -inis (f)	custom; way of life
***consul consulis** (m)	consul
consulatus -ūs (m)	consulship
contemno -ere contempsi contemptum	I despise, disregard
contingo -ere contigi contactum	I happen
contio -ionis (f)	public meeting, rally
***contra** (+ acc)	against
convalesco -ere -valui -valitum	I grow strong
conveho -ere -vexi -vectum	I transport
convenit -ire -venit -ventum	it is convenient
converto -ere -verti -versum	I turn
convoco -are -avi -atum	I summon
***corpus corporis** (n)	body
corrumpo -ere -rupi -ruptum	I bribe
***cotidie**	every day
credibilis -e	believable
***credo -ere credidi creditum** (+ dat)	I believe
***crimen criminis** (n)	accusation, charge; guilt

*crudelis -e	cruel
cruentus -a -um	bloodstained
crux crucis (f)	cross, crucifixion
*cum	since; when; although
*cum (+ abl)	with
*cunctus -a -um	the whole, all
cupiditas -tatis (f)	desire
*cupio -ere cupivi cupitum	I desire, want
*cur	why
curia -ae (f)	senate-house
custodia -ae (f)	protection
*de (+ abl)	about; down from
*debeo -ēre -ui -itum	I owe; I ought, have to
debilis -e	feeble
decempeda -ae (f)	measuring-rod
decimus -a -um	tenth
declaro -are -avi -atum	I declare, make clear
dedo -ere dedidi deditum	I give up, surrender
deduco -ere -duxi -ductum	I lead down, bring down
*defendo -ere defendi defensum	I defend
defensio -ionis (f)	defence
defensor -oris (m)	defender
defero deferre detuli delatum	I report
deicio -ere -ieci -iectum	I cast out, remove
*dein, deinde	then
delecto -are -avi -atum	I delight
delicatus -a -um	delicate
demens dementis	insane
*denique	finally
denuntio -are -avi -atum	I threaten

depello -ere -puli -pulsum	I drive back, get rid of
depopulor -ari -atus	I devastate
derivo -are -avi -atum	I divert, deflect, avoid
describo -ere -scripsi -scriptum	I describe, mean
desidero -are -avi -atum	I miss
desilio -ire -silui -sultum	I leap down
***despero -are -avi -atum**	I despair (of), lose hope
deus dei (m)	god
deverto -ere -verti -versum	I divert, detour; I break my journey
***dextera -ae** (f) (*or* dextra)	right hand
di	*pl of* **deus**
***dico -ere dixi dictum**	I say
dictator -oris (m)	dictator, mayor
dictito -are -avi -atum	I say, keep saying
***dies diei** (m)	day
***difficilis -e**	difficult
***dignitas -tatis** (f)	rank, position
***dignus -a -um** (+ abl)	worthy (of), deserving
dilacero -are -avi -atum	I tear apart
dilectus -ūs (m)	selection
diluo -ere dilui dilutum	I wash away, refute
***dimitto -ere -misi -missum**	I dismiss, bring to an end
disputo -are -avi -atum	I argue
dissimulo -are -avi -atum	I pretend
***diu** (*comparative* **diutius**)	for a long time
diuturnus -a -um	long-lasting, enduring
dius fidius	god of truth
me dius fidius	by all that is true, 'I swear'
divinus -a -um	divine, god-given
***do dare dedi datum**	I give
***doceo -ēre docui doctum**	I teach; I explain

doctus -a -um	learned, intelligent
***dolor -oris** (m)	pain; resentment
dominor -ari -atus	I rule, am in total control
***dominus -i** (m)	master, owner, slave-owner
domitor -oris (n)	conqueror
***domus -ūs** (f) (*irreg*)	house, home
***dubito -are -avi -atum**	I doubt; I hesitate
***duco -ere duxi ductum**	I lead, take, bring, extend
***dum**	while; (*with subjunctive*) until
***dux ducis** (m)	leader
***e, ex** (+ abl)	from, out of
eculeus -i (m)	rack (instrument of torture)
editus -a -um	high
educo -ere eduxi eductum	I bring out, draw
***efficio -ere effeci effectum**	I bring it about, make (something happen)
efflo -are -avi -atum	I breathe out
effrenatus -a -um	unrestrained, frenzied
***effugio -ere -fugi -fugitum**	I escape, avoid
***ego**	I
***egredior -i egressus**	I go out
eligo -ere elegi electum	I choose
eludo -ere elusi elusum	I have free rein, do whatever I want
emolumentum -i (n)	advantage, inducement
***enim**	for
enitor -i enisus	I strive, struggle
***eques equitis** (m)	equestrian (a rank in Roman society)
equidem	indeed, actually
***equus -i** (m)	horse

*erga (+ acc)	(feelings) towards
*ergo	therefore
eripio -ere -ripui -reptum	I snatch away
erumpo -ere erupi eruptum	I break out
*et	and
*et ... et ...	both ... and ...
etenim	in fact
*etiam	also; even, actually; still
*etsi	even if, although
everto -ere everti eversum	I overturn, overthrow
evoco -are -avi -atum	I summon up
evomo -ere evomui evomitum	I pour out
exanimatus -a -um	weakened, frightened
excelsus -a -um	high, raised
*excito -are -avi -atum	I rouse, raise
exeo exire exii exitum	I go out, leave
exercitatio -ionis (f)	exercising, scope
*exercitus -ūs (m)	army
existimo -are -avi -atum	I think, believe
*exitium -ii (n)	destruction
exitus -ūs (m)	result, outcome
exoletus -i (m)	(male) prostitute
exopto -are -avi -atum	I long for
expeditus -a -um	unencumbered, travelling light
expello -ere -puli -pulsum	I drive away/from
expers expertis (+ gen)	remote from
expeto -ere -petii -petitum	I look for, expect, require
expio -are -avi -atum	I placate, appease (the gods), offer as appeasement
expleo -ēre explevi expletum	I satisfy
expono -ere -posui -positum	I explain
exsisto -ere exstiti	I turn out (to be)

*exspecto -are -avi -atum	I wait (for)
exstinguo -ere -stinxi -stinctum	I wipe out
exstruo -ere -struxi -structum	I construct
exsulto -are -avi -atum	I gloat
extermino -are -avi -atum	I banish
exterus -a -um	foreign
extimesco -ere extimui	I am terrified, am appalled
extremus -a -um	at the end
*facilis -e	easy
*facinus facinoris (n)	deed; crime
*facio -ere feci factum	I do, I make
factum -i (n)	deed
facultas -tatis (f)	opportunity
*fallo -ere fefelli falsum	I escape the notice of, am mistaken by
falsus -a -um	false, untrue
familiaris -is (c)	friend, associate (*adj used as noun*)
res familiaris	personal property, wealth
fas (n) (*indecl*)	(what is) right
fateor -ēri fassus	I admit
fatum -i (n)	fate, destiny
Februarius -a-um	of February
*femina -ae (f)	woman
*fere	almost, more or less
*fero ferre tuli latum	I carry; I endure; I pass a law (for)
*ferrum -i (n)	iron; sword
ferus -a -um	wild
festinatio -ionis (f)	haste
*fidelis -e	faithful

fidus -a -um	reliable, firm
fingo -ere finxi fictum	I create, invent, imagine
***fio fieri factus sum**	I become
***fit**	it happens
flamen -inis (m)	priest
fons fontis (m)	fountain; source
***fortasse**	perhaps
***fortis -e**	brave
***fortuna -ae** (f)	fortune, fate
***forum -i** (n)	forum
***frango -ere fregi fractum**	I break
***frater fratris** (m)	brother
fraus fraudis (f)	criminal behaviour
freno -are -avi -atum	I control
fruor frui fruitus (+ abl)	I enjoy
fundamentum -i (n)	foundation
fundus -i (m)	estate
furiosus -a -um	wild, crazy
furo -ere furui	I behave wildly
***furor -oris** (m)	wild behaviour
***gaudium -ii** (n)	joy
***gens gentis** (f)	people, nation
germanus -a -um	with the same parents, very own
***gero -ere gessi gestum**	I manage, hold (an office); (*in passive*) happen
***gladius -ii** (m)	sword
gloria -ae (f)	glory
gloriose	boastfully
gradus -ūs (m)	stage, level; status
Graeculus -a -um	Greek (*contemptuous diminutive*)

*gratia -ae (f)	thanks; friendship
grex gregis (m)	flock, herd, company
guberno -are -avi -atum	I manage, direct
*habeo -ēre -ui -itum	I have, hold
haereo -ēre haesi haesum	I cling; I come to grief
harena -ae (f)	sand
heres heredis (c)	heir
heus	hey!
*hic	here
*hic haec hoc	this; he, she, it
*homo hominis (c)	man, person
honestus -a -um	honest
*honos honoris (m) (*or* honor)	honour; political office
*hora -ae (f)	hour
*hortus -i (m)	garden
hostis hostis (c)	enemy
*iaceo -ēre -ui -itum	I lie down; I am refuted, disproved
iactura -ae (f)	loss; spending
*iam	(by) now, already
*idem eadem idem	the same
*igitur	therefore
ignarus -a -um (+ gen)	ignorant of, unaware of
*ignoro -are -avi -atum	I do not know
ignotus -a -um	unknown
*ille illa illud	that; he, she, it
imago imaginis (f)	picture
imbutus -a -um	tainted (with)
immitto -ere -misi -missum	I let loose
immo	on the contrary
immortalis -e	immortal

immortalitas -tatis (f)	immortality
imparatus -a -um	unprepared
impedimenta -orum (n) (pl)	baggage
impeditus -a -um	encumbered; cumbersome, restrictive, sluggish
impello -ere impuli impulsum	I drive
impendeo -ēre	I threaten
***imperator -oris** (m)	general, commander
imperitus -a -um	unskilled, unknowledgeable, uncommitted
imperium -ii (n)	power
impetro -are -avi -atum	I gain, succeed in getting
***impetus -ūs** (m)	charge, attack
impleo -ēre implevi impletum	I fill
imprimo -ere -pressi -pressum	I press on; I write down, record
improbus -a -um	wicked
impune	without being punished, freely
impunitas -tatis (f)	not being punished, impunity
***in**	(+ *acc*) into, against, towards
	(+ *abl*) in, on, in the case of
in dies	day by day
inanis -e	empty, imaginary
***incendo -ere incendi**	I burn
incensum	
incertus -a -um	uncertain, unclear
incido -ere -cidi -casum	I fall among, fall under
***incipio -ere -cepi -ceptum**	I begin
incorruptus -a -um	honest, unbiassed
incredibilis -e	extraordinary, amazing
indico -are -avi -atum	I point to, accuse, give away
indignus -a -um	unworthy; undeserved, demeaning

inferi -orum (m) (pl)	those below, the dead
***infero inferre intuli inlatum**	I bring in, carry, use; I raise
inflammatus -a -um	burning
ingressus -ūs (m)	entry
inimicitiae -arum (f pl)	hostility
inimicus -i (m)	enemy; (*as adj.*) hostile
***iniuria -ae** (f)	harm, wrongdoing, grievance
iniuriā (abl)	without justification
iniustus -a -um	unjust
inlecebra -ae (f)	temptation, inducement
***inquam**	I say
inretio -ire -ivi -itum	I ensnare
inruo -ere inrui	I charge (at), make an attack
insanus -a -um	wild; ridiculous
inscitia -ae (f)	inexperience, incompetence
***insidiae -arum** (f pl)	ambush, trap
insidiator -oris (m)	ambusher, highwayman
insidior -ari -atus (+ dat)	I ambush
insidiosus -a -um	dangerous
inspecto -are -avi -atum	I watch
instituo -ere institui institutum	I begin; I establish
***insula -ae** (f)	island
integer -gra -grum	complete, whole; pure, upright
***intellego -ere -lexi -lectum**	I understand, realise
Interamnanus -a -um	of Interamna
intercludo -ere -clusi -clusum	I close off, cut off
interdum	sometimes
intereo -ire -ii -itum	I die
interest (+ gen)	it matters (to)
interfector -oris (m)	killer
***interficio -ere -feci -fectum**	I kill
***interim**	meanwhile

interitus -ūs (m)	death
interpono -ere -posui -positum	I make (myself) a negotiator, I negotiate
intueor -ēri intuitus	I look upon
*invenio -ire inveni inventum	I find
invidia -ae (f)	jealousy; unpopularity
*invitus -a -um	unwilling
*ipse ipsa ipsum	himself, herself, itself; myself etc (*emphatic*)
*ira irae (f)	anger
*iratus -a -um	angry
*is ea id	he, she, it; this; that
iste ista istud	this, that; your
*ita	in such a way
*itaque	and so
item	likewise, similarly
*iter itineris (n)	journey
*iudex iudicis (m)	member of jury
iudicium -ii (n)	court; case, trial
iudico -are -avi -atum	I judge
iugulo -are -avi -atum	I cut the throat
iugulum -i (n)	throat
iuror -ari iuratus	I swear, state under oath
ius iuris (n)	law, justice, legality, rights
iure (abl)	justifiably
*iustus -a -um	just; justified
Kalendae -arum (f pl)	the Calends (first of the month)
labefacto -are -avi -atum	I shake, weaken
lacrima -ae (f)	tear
lacus -ūs (m)	lake

laetitia -ae (f)	happiness, joy
Lanuvini -orum (m) (pl)	people of Lanuvium
largior -iri -itus	I grant
latro latronis (m)	robber
latum	*see* **fero**
*****laudo -are -avi -atum**	I praise
legitimus -a -um	required by law
*****lego -ere legi lectum**	I read; I choose
levo -are -avi -atum	I lighten, subsidise
*****lex legis** (f)	law
*****libenter**	gladly
*****liber libera liberum**	free
*****liberi -orum** (m) (pl)	children
*****libero -are -avi -atum**	I free; I acquit
*****libertas -tatis** (f)	freedom
libido -inis (f)	desire, lust
licentia -ae (f)	permission; lawlessness, anarchy
*****licet -ēre**	it is allowed
limen liminis (n)	threshold, doorway
linter lintris (f)	boat, barge
lis litis (f)	prosecution
*****locus -i** (m)	place
longinquus -a -um	distant
*****loquor -i locutus**	I speak
luceo -ēre luxi	I shine out
lupa -ae (f)	she-wolf; (female) prostitute
*****magis**	more (*advb*)
magistratus -ūs (m)	magistracy, political office
magnitudo -inis (f)	greatness
*****magnus -a -um**	great
maiores -um (m) (pl)	ancestors

*malus -a -um	bad
malum -i (n)	trouble
mancus -a -um	weak, crippled
*mando -are -avi -atum	I entrust
*mane	in the morning
*maneo -ēre mansi mansum	I remain, stay
*manus -ūs (f)	hand
manu mitto -ere misi missum	I free (a slave)
Mars Martis (m)	Mars; warfare, experience of war
materia -ae (f)	material, essence
materies -ei (f)	material
memoria -ae (f)	memory, record
*mens mentis (f)	mind
*mensis -is (m)	month
mentior -iri mentitus	I (tell a) lie
mercennarius -a -um	hired, in the pay of
mereor -ēri meritus	I earn, deserve; I have served
meritus -a -um	deserved
meritum -i (n)	good deed, service
metuo -ere metui metutum	I fear
*metus -ūs (m)	fear
*meus mea meum	my
mille	thousand
miliens	a thousand times
minime	not at all
*minor -ari minatus (+ dat of person)	I threaten
minus	less
mirifice	wonderfully, amazingly
misceo -ēre miscui mixtum	I mix; I cause confusion
*miser misera miserum	unhappy

*__modus -i__ (m)	method, way
__quem ad modum__	as far as; in what way, how?
*__modo__	only; just now
__non modo . . . sed etiam . . .__	not only . . . but also . . .
__moleste__	with difficulty
__moleste fero__	I resent, feel bad about
__mora -ae__ (f)	delay
*__morior mori mortuus__	I die
__mortuus -a -um__	dead
*__mors mortis__ (f)	death
*__mos moris__ (m)	custom
*__moveo -ēre movi motum__	I move
__muliebris -e__	womanly
*__mulier mulieris__ (f)	woman
__muliercula -ae__ (f)	weak woman (*diminutive*)
*__multus -a -um__	much
*__multi -ae -a__	many
*__muto -are -avi -atum__	I change
__mutus -a -um__	silent
*__nam__	for
__nanciscor -i nactus__	I obtain
*__nascor nasci natus__	I am born
__natio -ionis__ (f)	nation, people
*__natura -ae__ (f)	nature
*__-ne__	*indicates question*
*__ne__ (with subj)	in order that . . . not . . .; not (*in wishes*)
*__ne . . . quidem__	not even
*__nec, neque__	nor, and . . . not
*__nec (neque) . . . nec (neque)__	neither . . . nor . . .
__neque enim__	for . . . not

necessarius -a -um	necessary, unavoidable
*****necesse**	necessary
necessitas -tatis (f)	necessity
*****neco -are -avi -atum**	I kill
nefarius -a -um	wicked
nefas (n)	a forbidden act, crime
*****nego -are -avi -atum**	I deny: I say (that ...) not
*****negotium -ii** (n)	business; trouble
*****nemo** (*irreg decl*)	no-one, none
*****nescio -ire -ivi -itum**	I do not know
nescioquis -quis -quid	some
[**nex** *nom not found*] **necis** (f)	killing
*****nihil**	nothing
nimis	too much, excessively
*****nisi**	if ... not, unless; except
nobilis -e	noble, aristocratic
*****noctu**	at night
nocturnus -a -um	in the night
*****nolo nolle nolui**	I do not want; I refuse
*****non**	not
*****nondum**	not yet
*****nonnulli -ae -a**	some, a number of
nonnumquam	sometimes
*****nos**	we
*****noster nostra nostrum**	our
*****nosco -ere novi notum**	I get to know, know
noto -are -avi -atum	I blame
*****notus -a -um**	known
*****novus -a -um**	new, changed
*****nox noctis** (f)	night
nugae -arum (f pl)	nonsense
*****nullus -a -um**	no

*num	whether; surely ... not ...?
*numquam	never
*nunc	now
*nuntio -are -avi -atum	I announce, report
*nuntius -ii (m)	message
*ob (+ acc)	because of
quam ob rem	therefore
obduresco -ere obdurui	I grow hardened
obeo -ire -ii -itum	I meet, am on time for
*obliviscor -i oblitus	I forget
obscurus -a -um	unclear
obsigno -are -avi -atum	I sign as a witness
obsto -are obstiti obstatum (+ dat)	I am in the way, hinder
obsum obesse (+ dat)	I am an obstacle, hinder
*obviam fio/sum (+dat)	I meet, come face to face with
*occido -ere occidi occisum	I kill
occultator -oris (m)	concealer
*occupo -are -avi -atum	I seize
occurro -ere occurri occursum	I meet: I occur
*oculus -i (m)	eye
*odi odisse	I hate
*odium odii (n)	hatred
odio sum (+ dat)	I am hated (by)
*omitto -ere omisi omissum	I omit, do not mention
*omnino	completely, (not ...) at all
*omnis -e	every, all
opinio -ionis (f)	opinion
*opprimo -ere -pressi -pressum	I overwhelm
*[ops] (*only* opem *and* ope *exist in the singular*)	means, resources

optabilis -e	preferable
optatus -a -um	desirable
opto -are -avi -atum	I wish for
***opus operis** (n)	work
***opus est** (+ abl)	there is a need (of)
***oratio orationis** (f)	speech
orbis orbis (m)	circle
orbis terrarum	the world
oscito -are -avi -atum	I yawn, am half-asleep
***ostendo -ere ostendi ostentum**	I show
pactum -i (n)	agreement
quo pacto?	by what means, how?
***paene**	almost
paenula -ae (f)	heavy cloak
paenulatus -a -um	in a heavy cloak
***palam**	openly
paratus -a -um	prepared, ready
paries parietis (m)	wall
***pars partis** (f)	part; side, direction
partim	partly
partim ... partim ...	some ... others ...
partior -iri partitus	I share out
parum	too little
***parvus -a -um**	small
pateo -ēre patui	I lie open, am obvious
patientia -ae (f)	patience
***patior pati passus**	I suffer; I allow
patria -ae (f)	homeland, country
***paulisper**	for a short time
pecco -are -avi -atum	I do wrong
***pecunia -ae** (f)	money

**pello -ere pepuli pulsum	I drive
penes (+ acc)	in the hands of, under the control of
penetro -are -avi -atum	I penetrate, get as far as
penitus	deeply, thoroughly
*per (+ acc)	through; by
peragro -are -avi -atum	I travel over, go over
percallesco -ere percalui	I beome hardened, resigned
percello -ere perculi perculsum	I strike
percitus -a -um	excited, hot-headed
percutio -ere percussi percussum	I hit, shock
*perdo -ere perdidi perditum	I lose
perditus -a -um	immoral, depraved
perennis -e	undying
*pereo perire perii peritum	I die
perfero -ferre -tuli -latum	I endure
*periculum -i (n)	danger
permulti -ae -a	very many
perpetuus -a -um	constant, continued
persequor -i -secutus	I follow through, deal with
persolvo -ere -solvi -solutum	I pay
persona -ae (f)	character
perspicio -ere -spexi -spectum	I have a good look at
*perterritus -a -um	very frightened
petitio -ionis (f)	(election) campaign
*peto -ere petivi petitum	I seek, make for, target
pingo -ere pinxi pictum	I paint
placo -are -avi -atum	I calm
*plenus -a -um (+ gen *or* abl)	full
Plotius -a -um	of Plotius
plus	more

*poena -ae (f)	punishment
*populus -i (m)	people, nation
porro	however
portentum -i (n)	portent, omen, precedent
*posco -ere poposci	I demand
possessio -ionis (f)	possession, property
possideo -ēre possedi possessum	I take possession of
*possum posse potui	I am able
*post (+ acc)	after, behind (*sometimes adverb*)
*postremo	finally
*postridie	on the next day
*postulo -are -avi -atum	I demand
*potestas -tatis (f)	power
potissimus -a -um	most suitable
*potius	rather
potus -a -um	drunk
prae (+ abl)	in front of
prae se ferre	to display publicly, make no secret of
praecipuus -a -um	special
praeclarus -a -um	glorious
praedico -are -avi -atum	I proclaim, advertise
*praemium -ii (n)	reward
praescribo -ere -scripsi -scriptum	I command
praesens praesentis	present; alert
praesentia -ae (f)	presence; control
praesertim	particularly
*praesidium -ii (n)	protection, bodyguard
*praeter (+ acc)	except, apart from
*praetor -oris (m)	praetor

praetura -ae (f)	praetorship
pransus -a -um	well-fed, bloated
preces -um (f pl)	prayers, pleading
pridie	the day before
Prilius -a-um	Prilian (name of a small lake)
primum	firstly; for the first time
privatus -a -um	personal
privatus -i (m)	an ordinary citizen
privo -are -avi -atum	I deprive
***pro** (+ abl)	for
probo -are -avi -atum	I prove; I approve
prodo -ere -didi -ditum	I install
produco -ere -duxi -ductum	I produce
profectio -ionis (f)	setting out
***proficiscor -i profectus**	I set off
profecto	definitely
prohibeo -ēre -ui -itum	I prevent
proicio -ere -ieci -iectum	I throw in front, expose
promptus -a -um	suitable
***prope** (+ acc)	near; (*as adverb*) almost
propero -are -avi -atum	I hurry
properato (*abl of abstract noun*)	haste
propinquus -a -um	near
propono -ere -posui -positum	I put forward, offer, imagine
***propter** (+ acc)	because of
propulso -are -avi -atum	I repel, beat off
prosum prodesse profui (+dat)	I benefit
***proximus -a -um**	next
proxime (+acc)	very near to
pubes pubis (f)	youth, young men
***publicus -a -um**	official, of the state, state-owned

pudicitia -ae (f)	decency
***pudor pudoris** (m)	morality
***puer pueri** (m)	boy
***pugna -ae** (f)	fight, fighting
***pugno -are -avi -atum**	I fight
pulvinar -aris (n)	(sacred) couch
punitor -oris (m)	punisher
purus -a -um	pure, guiltless
***puto -are -avi -atum**	I think
quadriduum -i (n)	four days
***quaero -ere quaesivi**	I look for; I ask (about),
quaesitum	investigate
quaeso	= **quaero**
quaestio -ionis (f)	(legal) enquiry, investigation,
	interrogation
***qualis -e**	what sort of?
***quam**	than; how (*exclamation*); (*with*
	superlative) as ... as possible
***quamquam**	although
***quantus -a -um**	how great
quanto ..., tanto ...	the more ..., the more ...
***-que**	and
queo -ivi -itum	I am able
***qui quae quod**	(*as pronoun*) who, which;
	(*as adjective*) who, what?; any
quicumque quaecumque	whoever, whatever
quodcumque	
qui?	how?
***quia**	because
***quidam quaedam quoddam**	a certain, some, a
***quidem**	indeed

quin	but that, without (...ing); (*beginning a sentence*) why ... not?
quin etiam	in actual fact
quippe	indeed, clearly
*quis quis quid	who? what?; anyone, anything (*pronoun*)
quid	why?
quisnam quaenam quidnam	whoever, whatever? what possible ...?
*quisque quidque	each, every
*quoad	until; as long as
quocumque	(to) wherever
*quod	because
*quod si	but if
*quoniam	since
*quoque	also
raeda -ae (f)	carriage
raedarius -ii (m)	coach driver
*rapio -ere rapui raptum	I seize, carry off
*ratio rationis (f)	reason, intelligence
ratiocinor -ari -atus	I calculate
*recens recentis	recent
recensio -ionis (f)	census
receptor -oris (m)	receiver
recordor -ari -atus	I remember
recurro -ere recurri recursum	I run back
*redeo -ire -ii -itum	I return
reditus -ūs (m)	return
regno -are -avi -atum	I rule, am a king
*regnum -i (n)	kingdom, kingship

reicio -ere -ieci -iectum	I throw off
religio -ionis (f)	religious barrier, technical difficulty; religious rite, religious status
***relinquo -ere reliqui relictum**	I leave, abandon
removeo -ēre -movi -motum	I remove
repello -ere reppuli repulsum	I drive back, resist
***repente**	suddenly
reprehendo -ere -di -sum	I criticise
reprimo -ere -pressi -pressum	I restrain, prevent
repugno -are -avi -atum	I fight against, oppose
***res rei** (f)	thing, matter
***res publica, rei publicae** (f)	the state
res novae (f pl)	revolution
resideo -ēre -sedi	I settle down
respiro -are -avi -atum	I breathe again
***respondeo -ēre -di -sum**	I answer
restituo -ere restitui restitutum	I restore
reus rea reum	defendant, on trial
revertor -i reverti reversum	I return
revivisco -ere revixi revictum	I come back to life
***rex regis** (m)	king
***ripa -ae** (f)	river bank
rogatio -ionis (f)	bill, proposed legislation
***rogo -are -avi -atum**	I ask
Romanus -a -um	Roman
sacramentum -i (n)	deposit (paid to a court)
sacrificium -ii (n)	sacrifice
***saepe**	often
***salus salutis** (f)	safety, survival

salutaris -e	beneficial, good, 'a blessing'
salvus -a -um	safe, preserved, acquitted
sanctus -a -um	holy
sane	in fact
***sanguis sanguinis** (m)	blood
***sapiens sapientis**	wise, sensible, intelligent
satio -are satiavi satiatum	I satisfy, please
***satis**	enough, sufficient
sceleratus -a -um	wicked
***scelus -eris** (n)	crime; wickedness
scilicet	indeed, obviously
***scio -ire scivi scitum**	I know
scortum -i (n)	prostitute
***scribo -ere scripsi scriptum**	I write
***se** (*sometimes* **sese**)	himself
secum	with himself
secus	differently
***sed**	but
sedeo -ēre sedi sessum	I sit
seditio -ionis (f)	disorder, uprising
seges segetis (f)	cornfield, soil
***semel**	(only) once
***semper**	always
sempiternus -a -um	everlasting
***senatus -ūs** (m)	senate
sensus -ūs (m)	feeling
***sententia -ae** (f)	opinion; vote
***sentio -ire sensi sensum**	I feel
separo -are -avi -atum	I separate, keep apart
sermo sermonis (m)	talk, conversation
***servo -are -avi -atum**	I save, rescue
***servus -i** (m)	slave

severus -a -um	severe, strict
***si**	if
***sic**	in this way, in the same way
sicarius -ii (m)	cutthroat, assassin
***sicut, sicuti**	just as
significo -are -avi -atum	I make clear
***signum -i** (n)	sign, indication, proof; (military) standard
***silva -ae** (f)	wood, forest
***simul**	at the same time; together with
sin	but if
***sine** (+ abl)	without
singularis -e	outstanding, extraordinary
singuli -ae -a	each one
sis = si vis	if you wish, 'please'
***sive ... sive ...**	whether ... or ...
***socius -ii** (m)	ally
***soleo -ēre solitus**	I am accustomed (to do), usually do
solitudo solitudinis (f)	loneliness
sollemnis -e	formal, religious
***solus -a -um**	alone
***solum**	only
non solum ... sed etiam ...	not only ... but also ...
***solvo -ere solvi solutum**	I free, acquit
solutus -a -um	unrestrained
***soror sororis** (f)	sister
sors sortis (f)	lot, allocation
***specto -are -avi -atum**	I look at/for
***spero -are -avi -atum**	I hope
***spes spei** (f)	hope, expectation; potential
splendidus -a -um	splendid, fine

spolio -are -avi -atum	I plunder, rob, strip a victim of his armour
***statim**	immediately
***statuo -uere -ui -utum**	I decide
status -a -um	fixed
stuprum -i (n)	(sexual) perversion
suadeo -ēre suasi suasum (+ dat)	I persuade; I urge, support
***subito**	suddenly
subsido -ere -sedi -sessum	I settle down, take up position
substructio -ionis (f)	foundations
succurro -ere -curri -cursum (+ dat)	I help
suffragatio -ionis (f)	support
suffragator -oris (m)	(political) supporter
suffragium -i (n)	vote
***sum esse fui**	I am
***summus -a -um**	greatest
summum	at most
superior -ius	previous; higher; with an advantage
***supero -are -avi -atum**	I overcome
supplicium -ii (n)	punishment
suspicio -ionis (f)	suspicion
***suspicor -ari -atus**	I suspect
sustineo -ēre -tinui -tentum	I withstand; I weaken, invalidate
***suus -a -um**	his/her (own)
symphoniacus -a -um	musical
tabula -ae (f)	tablet, document
***talis -e**	such
***tam**	so

*tamen	but, however
tamquam	as if
*tandem	at last; 'I ask you'
*tango -ere tetigi tactum	I touch, adjoin
*tantus -a -um	so great
*tantum	only
tardus -a -um	late
*tectum -i (n)	house
*telum -i (n)	weapon
tempto -are -avi -atum	I try, test; I attack
*tempus -oris (n)	time
*teneo -ēre tenui tentum	I hold; I remember
tergiversatio -ionis (f)	time-wasting
*tergum -i (n)	back, rear
termino -are -avi -atum	I limit
terminus -i (m)	limit, boundary
tertius -a -um	third
testamentum -i (n)	will
testimonium -ii (n)	evidence
testis -is (c)	witness
testor -ari testatus	I make my witness
tetrarches -ae (m)	tetrarch (a minor ruler)
*timeo -ēre -ui -itum	I fear
*timor timoris (m)	fear
tolerabilis -e	bearable
tormentum -i (n)	instrument of torture, torture
tortor -oris (m)	torturer
*tot	so many
*totus -a -um	whole
*trado -ere tradidi traditum	I hand over
*traho -ere traxi tractum	I drag, delay

*trans (+ acc)	across; on the other side of
transfero -ferre -tuli tralatum	I transfer, switch
tribunus -i plebis (m)	tribune of the people
tribuo -ere tribui tributum	I grant
tribus -ūs (f)	tribe (a voting unit)
triduum -i (n)	three days
*tristis -e	sad, gloomy, grim
trucido -are -avi -atum	I slaughter
tueor -ēri tuitus	I look over, protect
*tum	then
turbulentus -a -um	rowdy
tyrannus -i (m)	tyrant
*ubi	when; where
ultor ultoris (m)	avenger
umerus -i (m)	shoulder
*umquam	ever
*una	together, as well
*unde	from where (*also interrog*)
undecimus -a -um	eleventh
universus -a -um	entire
unus -a -um	one, only
*urbs urbis (f)	city
urgeo -ēre ursi	I put pressure on, trouble
usitatus -a -um	usual
*usus -ūs (m)	use; familiarity
*ut	(*with indicative*) as, when; although
	(*with subjunctive*) introduces purpose or result clause
*uter utra utrum	which (of two)?
*uterque utraque utrumque	each (of two), both

utilis -e	useful; advantageous
utilitas -tatis (f)	benefit
***utor uti usus** (+ abl)	I use, have the use of, have
***uxor uxoris** (f)	wife
***valeo -ēre -ui -itum**	I am strong; I am important, I count; I prevail
vehiculum -i (n)	vehicle
***vehor vehi vectus**	I ride
***vel**	or
vendo -ere vendidi venditum	I sell
***venio -ire veni ventum**	I come
***verbum -i** (n)	word; name
***vereor -ēri veritus**	I fear
versor -ari versatus	I am involved, am there
***verus -a -um**	true, real
re vera	truly, actually
***vero**	indeed
verum	but
***vesperi**	in the evening
***vester vestra vestrum**	your
but **vestrum** *also gen of* **vos**	
vestibulum -i (n)	entrance area
vestimentum -i (n)	garment (*in pl* clothes)
vestitus -ūs (m)	clothing
***vetus veteris**	old
vetustas -atis (f)	age, passing of time
vexator -oris (m)	one who harasses, interferes, disturbs; irritant
vexo -are -avi -atum	I harass, plague
***via viae** (f)	road
viator -oris (m)	traveller

vicissim	in turn
*victoria -ae (f)	victory
videlicet	obviously
*video -ēre vidi visum	I see
*videor	I seem
*villa -ae (f)	estate
*vinco -ere vici victum	I defeat
vindiciae -arum (f pl)	claim
violo -are -avi -atum	I treat violently, defile
*vir viri (m)	man
*virtus virtutis (f)	excellence; courage; (fine) character
*vis (*irreg decl*) (f)	force, violence, power
*vita -ae (f)	life
*vito -are -avi -atum	I avoid
*vivo -ere vixi victum	I live
*vivus -a -um	living
*vix	hardly
*volo velle volui	I want
*vos	you
votum -i (n)	prayer
*vox vocis (f)	voice; remark
*vulnus -eris (n)	wound
*vultus -ūs (m)	face, expression